Village

Che

G000108370

1

*This book is dedicated to
Anne and Richard Sommerville
in appreciation of their friendship.*

Village Walks
in
CHESHIRE

James F. Edwards

COUNTRYSIDE BOOKS
NEWBURY BERKSHIRE

First published 1997
© James F. Edwards 1997

All rights reserved.
No reproduction permitted without the prior
permission of the publisher:

COUNTRYSIDE BOOKS
3 Catherine Road
Newbury, Berkshire

ISBN 1 85306 457 2

Designed by Graham Whiteman
Photographs and maps by the author

Produced through MRM Associates Ltd., Reading
Printed by Woolnough Bookbinding Ltd., Irthlingborough

Contents

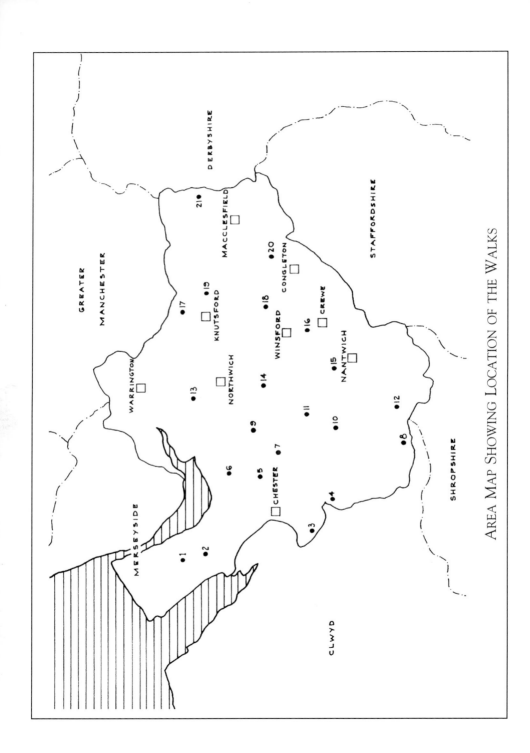

Area Map Showing Location of the Walks

WALK

Publisher's Note

We hope that you obtain considerable enjoyment from this book; great care has been taken in its preparation. Although at the time of publication all routes followed public rights of way or permitted paths, diversion orders can be made and permissions withdrawn.

We cannot of course be held responsible for such diversion orders and any inaccuracies in the text which result from these or any other changes to the routes, nor any damage which might result from walkers trespassing on private property. However, we are anxious that all details covering the walks are kept up to date and would therefore welcome information from readers which would be relevant to future editions.

Introduction

From the hills of the Peak District National Park in the east, across the central plain and shores of the Wirral Peninsula to the hills of Wales in the west; Cheshire is a county with rich and varied countryside.

The walks described in this book have been designed to give a taste of this variety whilst at the same time concentrating upon some of the more interesting villages within the county.

The roots of the majority of Cheshire's villages were set down hundreds of years ago at a time when communication was in its infancy. Villagers rarely travelled more than a few miles from their homes with the result that villages and hamlets retained a certain amount of individuality. Hence, there are always different types of architecture and settings to observe when passing through a particular village, for each has its own innate character.

This brings us to the motor car. The life-blood of any village is its inhabitants, and Cheshire has an abundance of villagers who really care for their environment. Therefore, readers are asked to respect the villagers' way of life and to use the utmost discretion when parking vehicles. Car parking locations are indicated in the text – but if they are full, or for some reason unusable, please ensure that you park your vehicle in such a way as not to be a nuisance to those who live close by. Many of the walks commence from the village inn where, it must be stressed, parking is only for patrons. What this means is that, provided you will be having food and drink at the inns, the landlords have agreed that vehicles can remain parked whilst patrons complete their walks.

Places of interest within striking distance of each individual village are given for each walk. Many of these attractions are visited on walks contained within a previous book – *Short Walks from Cheshire Pubs* – which is also published by Countryside Books. The time span covered by the attractions goes from the Roman remains at Chester, through the splendid halls of Arley, Tatton and Gawsworth, the Industrial Revolution at Quarry Bank Mill and the 20th-century motor museum at Mouldsworth to the futuristic fascination of Jodrell Bank where the wonders of the universe unfold. An entrance charge is payable for many of the attractions but you can learn so much about the county and its history by visiting them.

Places where food and drink can be obtained are also given for each walk. Opening times have not been included due to the fact that they can often change. However, these can always be obtained by using the telephone number which is given at the end of each description. Also, where the menu is the subject of constant variation, only an outline of the type of food available is given. Again, each place can be contacted in order to obtain specific menu details.

What you put on your feet is important. Waterproof walking shoes or boots are recommended, preferably worn over woollen socks. Smooth-soled shoes should not be worn as they can cause accidents and make walking hard work, especially after wet weather. Lightweight waterproof clothing should always be carried to combat the variable English weather. A small rucksack can be useful for carrying such items as food, cameras, binoculars and the like, which help to make a walk that much more enjoyable.

A prime objective has been to provide direct, no-nonsense route descriptions for each walk, coupled with a clear accompanying sketch map. For those requiring more detail, the relevant OS Landranger 1:50,000 map numbers are given (note that Sheet 118, titled 'Stoke-on-Trent' here, is named 'The Potteries' in earlier editions of the series). Do not be afraid to venture out during the winter months, for an excursion on a cold, clear day when frost has hardened the ground underfoot can be most rewarding, especially when coupled with a warming drink and a hearty meal taken in pleasant surroundings. However, if you wish to enjoy the facilities of an inn following the completion of a walk please remember to leave muddy walking boots in your car.

Finally, some words of thanks. As with previous surveys I have been accompanied during the preparations for this book by my mother who is an excellent walking companion, and has a discerning eye which brought to my attention many things I would otherwise have missed. For her helpful comments and suggestions, I am most grateful. Once again, the task of deciphering my handwriting and converting it into a typed manuscript was expertly carried out by Kath Mannion. I must also thank all the managers of the various inns, restaurants and teashops for taking time from their busy schedules in order to answer my many questions. And last, but by no means least, I met some extremely kind and interesting folk – the villagers of Cheshire.

James F. Edwards

THORNTON HOUGH

Length : 3 miles

Getting there: Thornton Hough straddles the B5136 road 2 miles from junction 4 of the M53 motorway and 3 miles from Neston.	Parking: There are numerous parking places in and around the village and patrons' parking at the Seven Stars Inn.	Map: OS Landranger – Liverpool (108) (GR 305810).

Thornton Hough possesses a most attractive village green which covers an area of some 14 acres and is surrounded by mock-Elizabethan, half-timbered black and white houses. There is a smithy, a post office and two churches, one of which carries an unusual fifth clock face set high on its northern aspect below the spire. This was installed by Joseph Hirst, a Yorkshire mill owner who was responsible for building part of the village during the 1860s and wanted to see the church clock from his bedroom window. Much of the remainder of the village was completed by the first Lord Leverhulme following his establishment of the well-known soap factory at Port Sunlight.

The walk links Thornton Hough with

the intriguing hamlet of Brimstage – where a fortified medieval hall and its adjacent courtyard have been developed into a range of imaginatively presented shops and craft outlets. Between the two places the route takes you through the attractive rich farming country of mid-Wirral along tracks and tree-lined paths.

THE WALK

❶ From the Seven Stars Inn cross the road and enter a broad track where a footpath sign points towards Brimstage. The track begins at the side of Thornton Hough primary school; it leads past a farm and then becomes a macadam lane between hedgerows. On meeting a junction turn right and after 45 yards turn left to follow a hedged-in path which skirts the Leverhulme estate.

❷ Cross a stile and follow a field edge, keeping a hedgerow on your immediate right. After 65 yards go over another stile and follow the next field edge with a hedgerow now on your immediate left. At the field corner keep on past a group of Scots pines to follow a well-defined path

---

PLACES of INTEREST

The model village of **Port Sunlight** is just 4 miles from Thornton Hough on the other side of the M53 motorway close to junction 4. It was constructed by the first Lord Leverhulme who was responsible for much of the building of Thornton Hough. The adjacent Lady Lever Art Gallery houses an outstanding collection of English 18th-century paintings, furniture and Leverhulme's world famous collection of Pre-Raphaelite paintings and Wedgwood (tel: 0151 644 6466).

---

across the next field. Pass over a tree-lined drive via a pair of metal kissing-gates and follow the path as it bears diagonally right across the next field.

Over to the left can be seen Thornton Manor. The manor, which was purchased by the first Lord Leverhulme in 1891, is the current home of the third Lord Leverhulme.

❸ Go over a stile at the side of a tree and follow a field edge for about 100 yards and then cross another stile to enter a tree-lined path. Arrive at a junction of paths. Keep forward here, in the same direction as before. The path emerges at a crossing road where the way is right. There is a junction of roads here. Keep right in the direction of Brimstage Hall and Craft Centre. Shortly, the road turns to the left but go over a stile on the right which is at the side of a large tree. A well-defined path leads across a field in the direction of a group of buildings which can be seen straight ahead. A stile in a crossing fence takes you into a car park close to the buildings.

The public footpath is forward and to the left of the buildings but bear right and then left to enter a large courtyard. At the

---

FOOD and DRINK

At the Seven Stars Inn a wide selection of pub food is available, including steaks, grills and various pies, seafood dishes, sandwiches, vegetarian dishes, and a fresh daily selection of sweets (tel: 0151 336 4574). The adjacent Village Stores Tea-room offers home-made cakes, scones, cream teas, crumpets, toast and a delicious selection of ice creams (tel: 0151 336 3719). Midway through the walk, at Brimstage Hall, is the Country Mouse Coffee Shop where freshly baked scones, cakes and pastries can be purchased (tel: 0151 342 5382).

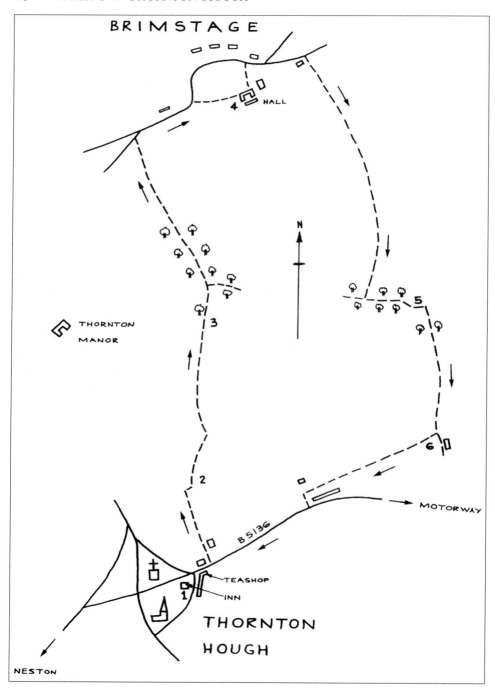

far side is the fortified medieval Brimstage Hall, with its imposing tower, whilst the buildings which form the courtyard contain a variety of speciality shops – including the Country Mouse Coffee Shop.

❹ On leaving the courtyard, follow the exit drive to arrive at a crossing road. Turn right to follow the roadside pavement and pass the village hall. Continue past Brimstage Lane, which goes off to the left, and then go over a stile on the right where a footpath sign points to Thornton Hough. Follow a field edge, keeping a stone wall and then a hedgerow on your immediate right. Pass over a drive via a pair of stiles and then bear left to another stile at the side of a gate. Follow the edge of the next field, keeping a hedgerow on your immediate left, cross a stile and continue now with a hedgerow on your immediate right. Pass over a tree-lined drive via a pair of stiles and follow a well-defined path across the next field. A gap in a crossing hedgerow leads onto a hedged-in path where the way is left.

❺ Emerge from the hedged-in path and pass over a tree-lined drive to enter a facing track. After only 30 yards, there is a junction of tracks where the way is right. Shortly, dwellings can be seen straight ahead. About 55 yards before reaching the dwellings leave the track and go over a stile on the right at the side of a field gate.

❻ Follow a path which hugs the field edge, keeping a hedgerow and trees on your immediate left. Go over a stile at the field corner and continue, as before, along the edge of the next field. Pass through a gap at the field corner to follow a broad grassy path which shortly takes you close to the gardens of dwellings which are on the left. A stile at the field corner gives access to a track where the way is left. Arrive at a crossing road and turn right to follow the roadside pavement back into Thornton Hough.

WILLASTON-IN-WIRRAL

Length : 3½ miles

Getting there: Willaston is on the B5133 8 miles to the north-west of Chester and 1 mile to the east of the A540 Chester to Hoylake road.

Parking: Drive down Hadlow Road – which is headed by signs telling you that Wirral Country Park is ¼ mile away – and arrive at a car park on the left adjacent to the old railway station. Alternatively, there is a car park closer to the village centre opposite Smithy Lane.

Map: OS Landranger – Chester (117) (GR 332772).

One of the oldest villages on the Wirral Peninsula, Willaston is a mix of the old and the new. At its heart is the village green, which is surrounded by former farmhouses and some more modern dwellings. Close by is the imposing Willaston Old Hall which was constructed during the 17th century and whose beautiful gardens are occasion-ally opened to the public during summer-time. The village also possesses a windmill, which dates from 1800 and has been converted into a private home. A short distance from the centre of the village is Hadlow Road Station which is now a feature on the Wirral Way, a linear park which links Hooton with West Kirby. The station – which closed during 1962 – has been restored to give the appearance of a typical day in 1952. A short length of track has been laid in front of the platform and there is a signal box, ticket office and various other trappings of the era.

Having absorbed the atmosphere of the 1950s at the station, the walk takes in a stretch of the Wirral Way prior to crossing a most attractive tract of undulating countryside along lanes, tracks and cross-country paths.

THE WALK

❶ From Hadlow Road Station cross Hadlow Road, where the original level-crossing gates still remain and follow a tree-lined footpath. The path runs along the course of the slightly raised embankment that once carried the railway lines. On the immediate left and running parallel to the footpath, there is a bridleway. After about $1/2$ mile, the two ways converge and you pass through a gap in a crossing wooden fence. About 100 yards further on, go under a bridge and continue.

❷ The path goes through a tree-lined cutting. Pass under a bridge. Shortly, the

---

PLACES of INTEREST

Just over $2^1/_2$ miles to the south-west of Willaston are the extensive 62 acre **Ness Gardens** which are a delight throughout all the seasons of the year (tel: 0151 353 0123).

---

path runs parallel to a lane on the immediate left and then converges with the lane just before a substantial concrete bridge. Go under the bridge and then keep to the right to follow a path which remains parallel to the lane. The lane turns away to the left, but keep forward along the footpath. The embankment is more pronounced in this area where there are glimpses of the surrounding fields. Cross a bridge which has substantial wooden railings on either side.

❸ Leave the embankment to the left now, where a sign says 'Cuckoo Lane to Little Neston'. Descend to arrive onto a lane via a stile. Turn right to follow the lane away from the bridge you have just walked over. About 150 yards further on there are a number of gates. Go through the facing gate to climb gradually along a rough sandy track between hedgerows.

Where the track levels out there are long views to the hills of Wales straight ahead. The track now turns to the right, but turn left, to go over a stile set at the side of a stone gatepost.

❹ Keep along a field edge where there is a fence and hedgerow on your immediate right. Go over a stile at the field corner and follow a fenced-in path. On crossing a further stile arrive on a track close by

---

FOOD and DRINK

Willaston has two fine inns: the Nag's Head and Pollard Inn. The Nag's Head, which dates from 1733, serves a wide selection of meals, snacks and sandwiches together with a comprehensive range of sweets. There is also a specials board to further tempt the palate (tel: 0151 327 2439). The Pollard Inn, formerly a farmhouse, is a roomy establishment boasting a large restaurant where meals with all the trimmings can be enjoyed. There is also a cocktail bar (tel: 0151 327 4615).

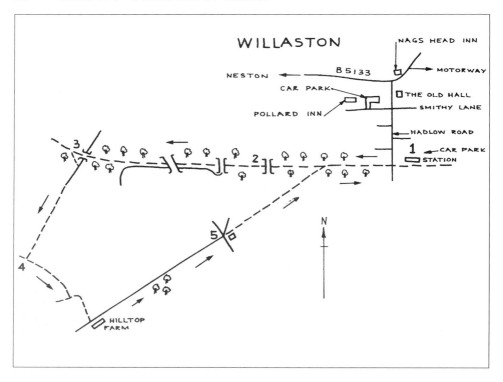

Windle Hill Nature Reserve. Turn left along the track. After a further 55 yards the track bends to the right and leads to a crossing lane opposite Hilltop Farm. Turn left along the lane and, after $1/2$ mile, arrive at a crossing road.

❺ Go straight across the road, taking care as it is usually quite busy. A facing stile at the side of a dwelling leads onto a short length of fenced-in path. On crossing another stile you have entered a very large field. Navigational care is now required because you must cross the field in the same direction as the short length of fenced-in path you have just negotiated. In just over $1/4$ mile the path converges with a fence on the other side of which are trees. A stile in the fence gives access to the Wirral Way. Turn right and retrace part of your initial route back to Hadlow Road Station less than $1/2$ mile away.

PULFORD

Length : 6 miles

Getting there: The village of Pulford straddles the B5445 midway between Chester and Wrexham.	Parking: If you are visiting the Grosvenor-Pulford Hotel then you may park in their car park. If not, then there	are parking places in and around the village. Map: OS Landranger – Chester (117) (GR 375587).

Pulford is on the very border between England and Wales. This strategic location meant that in medieval times a castle was built here, originally of wood but replaced by a stone building during the 13th century. Unfortunately, all that remains of this building is a mound in the field next to the churchyard. The Duke of Westminster owns much of the land in the area and the second Duke was responsible for rebuilding the church in cruciform shape with a tower and spire and a peal of six bells which are still rung to this day. Many of the dwellings in and around the village were also built by the second Duke and are constructed in a distinctive style from hand-made bricks which have been used to form Dutch gables and spiral chimneys.

From Pulford, the walk takes you across fields to the tiny hamlet of Darland before striking out across undulating agricultural pastures on the way to Poulton. The return journey follows a scenic track leading to the banks of a large drainage dyke which abounds with wildlife. Cross-country paths lead back to Darland prior to the return to Pulford.

THE WALK

❶ On leaving the Grosvenor-Pulford Hotel turn right and follow the roadside pavement to cross a sturdy stone bridge which carries the road over Pulford Brook and into Wales.

Enter the precincts of the village of Lavister and about 200 yards after crossing the stone bridge go over a stile on the left which is opposite the first dwelling on the right – a small bungalow. Cross a field to where, after 100 yards, you cross over a water-filled dyke via a flat bridge. Follow a well-defined path now which runs straight for about 550 yards and leads towards facing trees. On meeting the trees a stile at the side of a gate and cattle-grid takes you

---

PLACES of INTEREST

Less than 2 miles to the north of Pulford, and close to where the B5445 joins the A483 at Belgrave, is the **Grosvenor Garden Centre** where there is a sensory garden, water features, various displays and a coffee shop (tel: 01244 682856).

---

onto a lane. Follow the lane, where there are glimpses of a large pond through the trees on the left, to arrive at a crossing lane – where the way is left. This is the tiny hamlet of Darland. Pass dwellings, including the picturesque Darland Hall Cottage and arrive at a junction of ways just after passing a pond on the right. The lane bears to the right here but walk forward and turn left in front of a dwelling called The Elms to go over a stile at the right-hand side of a gate.

❷ Follow a rough track for 100 yards and then turn right to follow a path which hugs a hedgerow on the immediate right. After only 80 yards cross a stile and turn left to walk across a rough pasture. After 110 yards go over a stile at the left-hand side of a field gate. Bear right now, keeping a hawthorn hedge on your immediate right. After a further 100 yards bear left and walk to a footbridge you will see across the field about 220 yards away, at the rear of which can be seen a farm situated on higher ground. Cross the footbridge, which takes you over a water-filled dyke, and turn right. Bear left now and then climb, to go over a stile which is 10 yards to the right of a tree and at the side of a hedgerow.

❸ Walk forward along a field edge, keeping the hedgerow on your immediate

---

FOOD and DRINK

The origins of the Grosvenor-Pulford Hotel go back to the 18th century; however, the establishment has been modernised during recent years and now offers a high standard of food and drink. The bar area is light and airy and the welcome is warm and friendly. A wide range of bar snacks are on offer, including the All Day Grosvenor Breakfast and a good selection of sweets. There is also a daily specials board. Apart from bar snacks the hotel has a large restaurant set out in the Victorian style. Accommodation can also be provided if required (tel: 01244 570560).

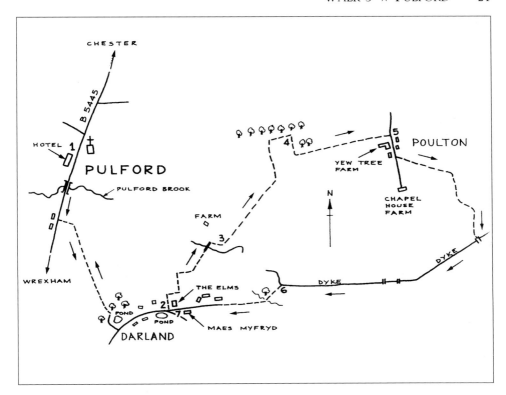

right. After 90 yards follow the hedgerow as it kinks to the left. Keep on past a stile on the right to follow the edge of a large field, keeping the hedgerow on your immediate right. At the field corner keep forward over a facing stile and keep on, in the same general direction as before, with a hedgerow on your immediate right. Follow the hedgerow as it bends to the left. You are now walking in the direction of trees which can be seen about 220 yards away straight ahead. Arrive close to the trees and turn right to go over a stile. Follow a track which stays parallel with the trees and after 165 yards arrive at a stile on the left. Navigational care is now required.

❹   Turn right, and with the stile at your back, walk across a rough pasture to the right of a small copse about 130 yards away. Pass the copse (which contains a pond) and after a further 30 yards turn left to arrive at an old metal gate. Pass through the gate and continue along the edge of a huge field keeping a hedgerow on the immediate left. Farm buildings can be seen about 550 yards ahead. On nearing the field corner there are the foundations of buildings long-since removed. Go over a stile at the field corner and follow a facing concrete drive. A facing gate gives access to a short length of hedged-in track. A stile at the side of the next gate takes you onto a lane in the hamlet of Poulton, where the way is right.

❺ Pass Yew Tree Farm, and a dwelling which was constructed in 1920, to arrive at the facing entrance drive of Chapel House Farm. Bear left here through a gate, to follow a hedged-in track where a footpath sign points towards Trevalyn. Follow the track through pleasant country-side and, after ³/₄ mile, go over a water-filled dyke via a sturdy stone bridge. Immediately on crossing the bridge turn right to walk along the elevated left-hand banking of the dyke. The dyke, and its environs, are a haven for many different species of wild fowl. After about 450 yards go over a fence-stile and continue along the edge of the dyke. Pass over another fence-stile, where there is a bridge on the right, and continue. Keep on past another bridge and after a further 650 yards arrive at a facing field gate. Leave the side of the dyke here and go over a stile down the banking on the left about 5 yards from the field gate.

❻ With the stile at your back, bear diagonally to the left and cross a rough field to go through a gate at the opposite field corner. Turn left now to pass over a bridge which takes you across a tree-lined stream. Bear diagonally right and walk across the next field, aiming just to the left of a dwelling which can be seen about 450 yards away across the field. Pass through a pair of facing gates and walk along a walled-in track which takes you to the left of the dwelling. Pass through another gate; there is a farmyard and outbuilding on the right here, but keep forward through another gate. Pass a dwelling on the left called Maes Myfryd to arrive at a junction of ways. On the right, in front of The Elms is the stile which you crossed earlier in the walk.

❼ Follow the facing lane through the hamlet of Darland and turn next right to retrace part of your initial route back to Pulford.

CHURTON

Length : 4 miles

Getting there: The B5130 runs due south connecting Chester with Farndon. Churton, just over 1 mile from Farndon, straddles this road.	Parking: If you are visiting the village pub, the White Horse Inn, then you may park in their car park. If not, then there are parking places in	and around the village. Map: OS Landranger – Chester (117) (GR 417565).

Churton is situated close by the Welsh border in the midst of some beautiful countryside. The border is formed by the river Dee whose waters flow less than a mile from the village centre and where, in days gone by, a flat-bottomed punt ferried travellers between the two countries. The village boasts an Elizabethan manor house opposite which, in the aptly named Pump Lane, there is an old water pump – one of several used to supply domestic water up to the 1930s. Churton has an interesting mix of dwellings and on one of the older houses, dated 1650, can be seen an exposed gable-end cruck frame.

The first half of the walk is along lanes and cross-country paths where there are splendid views to the Peckforton Hills. The greater part of the return leg takes in a bridleway which, during medieval times, was a well-used thoroughfare.

THE WALK

❶ Enter Hob Lane, which commences at the side of the White Horse Inn. Pass the tiny Churton Methodist church and arrive at a junction. There is a lane which goes off to the right and straight ahead a track, but turn left here to follow a lane which takes you past a mixture of dwellings. On passing The Knowl, a road which goes off to the left, the lane is hedged-in. Pass isolated dwellings and arrive at a crossing road. Turn left and follow the roadside pavement. After 200 yards turn right, cross the road and go over a stile to enter a large field.

❷ Bear right and walk across the field to go over a stile about 220 yards away in a crossing hedgerow. Keep forward now and then stay parallel with a hedgerow on the left. Go through a gap at the field corner, where there is a hedged-in track going off to the right, and keep forward to follow a well-defined path across the next field. Over to the right can be seen the needle-sharp structure of the Barnston Memorial –

FOOD and DRINK

The White Horse Inn serves delicious meals every lunchtime and during the evening. Home cooking is the order of the day here and there are starters, main courses and sweets to suit every taste. Light snacks, sandwiches and children's meals can also be purchased and traditional Sunday lunches are a favourite with families. During summertime, when the weather is fine, barbecues are prepared in the adjacent garden (tel: 01829 270208).

PLACES of INTEREST

Four miles to the south-east of Churton, along a minor road which runs due south from Barton and the A534, is **Stretton Water Mill**. The mill, which was restored during 1975, is operated as a working museum (tel: 01606 41331).

---

built to commemorate the gallant actions of a local soldier, Major Roger Barnston, at the Relief of Lucknow in 1857.

❸ On reaching the far side of the field continue along the edge of the next field, keeping a hawthorn hedge on your immediate left. Go over a stile at the field corner, where the squat square tower of Farndon church can be seen over to the right, and continue along the next field edge. Shortly, the hedgerow on the left turns away to the left at a junction of paths.

❹ Turn left now to follow the hedgerow along the edge of a very large field. Where the hedgerow turns away to the left keep forward to go over a stile which can be seen to the left of a field gate straight ahead. Enter a lane and turn left. After about 90 yards arrive at a pair of gates on the right where a sign indicates Sibbersfield Lane Farm. Pass through the gates and follow a driveway which takes you to the left of a large barn. Go through two gates and walk forward, in the same direction as before, to follow a concrete drive. Pass through another gate and continue along the concrete drive. Straight ahead there are splendid views to the Peckforton Hills, which dominate the skyline.

❺ Where the concrete drive terminates,

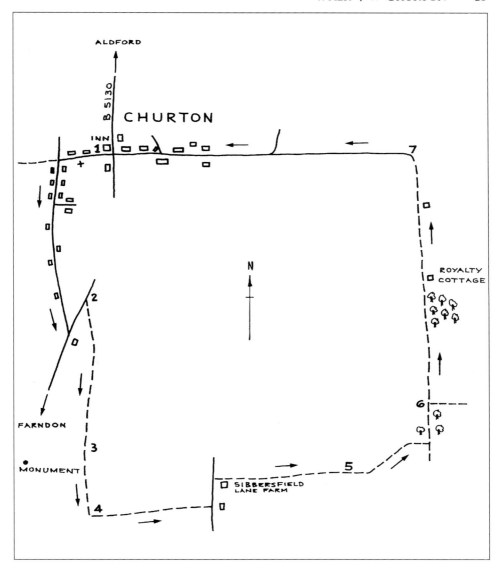

keep forward along a rough track which takes you into a field. Bear diagonally left now, cross the field and go over a plank-bridge and stile at the field corner. Keep along the edge of the next field where there is a fence, ditch and hedgerow on the immediate left. A small wooden gate and plank-bridge give access to a broad grassy track where the way is left.

❻ After about 150 yards keep forward, ignoring a track which goes off to the right, and pass through a facing gate to follow a hedged-in track. Continue past a small wood and a dwelling called Royalty Cottage. The going is along a rough gravel track now. Keep on, past a sandstone and brick dwelling and where the track terminates follow a narrow macadam lane which turns to the left.

❼   The lane takes you between hedgerows and emerges at a bend in a crossing lane. Keep left and follow the lane back into Churton village passing Church House (1682) and Churton Hall Farm with its adjacent water pump.

Churton Hall Farm

GREAT BARROW

Length : 4 miles

Getting there: Great Barrow is on the B5132 4 miles east of Chester and 1 mile north of the A51 Chester to Nantwich road.	Parking: There is a roadside parking strip at the side of the B5132 just to the south of Ferma Lane.	Map: OS Landranger – Chester (117) (GR 469685).

Situated at the southern end of Barrow Hill, Great Barrow is a pleasing mix of cottages and farmhouses, some dating back to the 17th century, whilst the sandstone tower of its half-hidden church has gazed out across the surrounding fields since 1744. A focal point at the village centre is an old water pump which was in use up to 1936 when piped water was installed.

The pump was restored during 1977 to celebrate the Queen's Silver Jubilee. The sandstone of the hill has been used to build numerous walls and a feature of the village is that many of its lanes are cut straight through the solid sandstone bedrock.

The walk takes you past the church, through the village centre, and along lanes and paths to the outlying district of

Broomhill. There is then a gradual climb to the outskirts of Little Barrow, where refreshment can be taken at the Foxcote Inn. A gentle descent across the northern slopes of Barrow Hill leads to a scenic track which brings you back to Great Barrow.

THE WALK

❶   On leaving the car, cross the road and enter a narrow lane which begins to the right of a dwelling called Hilltop. Arrive at St Bartholomew's church. There has been a church on this attractive site since 1291 and there is a complete list of rectors dating from 1313. The building was refurbished during the 1880s and contains items from the Victorian era. Keep to the right of the church to follow a grassy track around the edge of the raised church confines and then go through a gate on the left. A short straight path leads to the front of dwellings and then a track takes you to a crossing road. Turn right and then enter Mill Lane. The lane gradually descends past a mixture of dwellings old and new. About 20 yards before the lane crosses a bridge, go over a stile on the left. After only a further 20 yards, go over another stile to enter a field.

PLACES of INTEREST

Only 4 miles to the west of Great Barrow is the city of **Chester** – where 2,000 years of history have produced a legacy of Roman remains, a virtually complete circuit of medieval walls, 17th-century timber-framed houses and a cathedral and churches to rival any in England. There is also the river Dee to stroll beside and where pleasure craft can be hired during the summer months.

---

❷   Keep diagonally right at first and then bear left to follow the field edge along a path which stays close to a row of trees on the immediate right (there is a field on the other side of the trees which is at a lower level). The path leads to a stile near the field corner. Cross the stile and turn right to follow a lane. Pass Barrowmore Cottage and then turn next left shortly after passing Willow Cottage. Keep forward, passing a lane which goes off to the right at the side of Old Stone Cottage. Follow the lane to a T-junction and turn right in the direction of Tarvin and Oscroft. Where the lane turns sharply to the right, turn left, where a footpath sign points to Broomhill.

❸   Follow a track past a pair of cottages and then go over a plank-bridge and stile to enter a field. Bear slightly left now and after only 30 yards cross another stile. The path follows the edge of the next three fields, via stiles, where there are trees on the immediate right. Cross an open field next and go over another stile. Keep on, in the same general direction as before, and then go over a stile in a crossing fence.

❹   Turn left now to cross a stile at the side of a field gate in front of farm outbuildings.

FOOD and DRINK

The village pub, the White Horse, serves lunchtime and evening food together with a range of traditional ales. Halfway around the walk, the delightful Foxcote Inn provides a wide range of home-made meals seven days a week, lunchtime and evening. Daily specials are also available and children's portions are served. There are two bars, an outside play area and long views across the surrounding countryside (tel: 01244 301343).

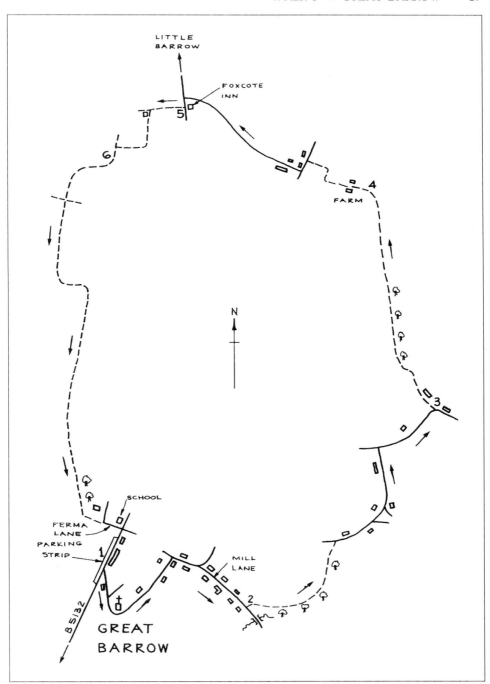

Walk forward here, to follow a track between the buildings. On the immediate left there is an old water pump. The track takes you to a crossing road where the way is left. After 65 yards, turn right to enter Broomhill Lane where a sign points towards Little Barrow. The lane gradually climbs and is a platform for long views to the right across to Helsby Hill. At the top of the climb there is a crossing road and the Foxcote Inn.

❺ Having taken some refreshment, enter a lane which commences opposite the inn. There are long views straight ahead here to Chester and the Welsh hills beyond. After 275 yards, and just before a bungalow on the left is reached, climb steps on the left to enter a large field. Follow the field edge, keeping a hedgerow on your immediate right. After a further 275 yards, follow the hedgerow as it turns to the right and gradually descend along the field edge. On reaching the bottom of the descent go over a facing stile and turn left to follow a narrow, hedged-in path.

❻ The path bends to the right and left – where it becomes a track. On meeting a junction of paths, with stiles on either side, keep forward to follow the track between hedges. The track bends to the left and right and then continues between fences. The track gradually climbs and is hedged in again prior to turning left past the entrance to the large black and white building of Greysfield. Keep forward now, passing a lane which goes off to the left, to follow the facing lane back into Great Barrow.

DUNHAM-ON-THE-HILL

Length : 6½ miles

Getting there: The village of Dunham-on-the-Hill lies just off the A56 Chester to Frodsham road midway between the two places. It is easily reached from the M56, being only 2 miles from junction 14, via the A5117 and A56 roads.

Parking: There are parking places in and around the village. There is also a large car park at the Wheatsheaf Inn (for patrons) which is situated at the northern end of the village by the A56 road.

Map: OS Landranger – Chester (117) (GR 473731).

As its name implies, Dunham-on-the-Hill is situated on a sandstone prominence overlooking the Mersey Estuary to the north and the Cheshire Plain to the south. There is an attractive village green with an old water pump and many picturesque cottages and other interesting dwellings. Several houses dating from the 16th and 17th century still exist and are sturdily constructed of sandstone with wattle and daub interior walls. The main village street, which was once part of the Chester to Warrington road, cuts through solid sandstone bedrock as it descends to its successor, the A56.

A mixture of field paths, tracks and

lanes, the walk initially heads east and cuts across agricultural land to Abbot's Clough. The route then heads towards Manley before turning south and then west to Long Green – from where a series of cross-country paths lead back to Dunham-on-the-Hill.

THE WALK

❶ Go over a stile directly opposite the exit drive of the Wheatsheaf Inn. Follow the edge of five fields, keeping a hedge-row on your immediate right, and pass over five stiles en-route. On reaching the end of the fifth field turn right through a gate and continue with a hedgerow now on your immediate left. A dwelling can be seen about 300 yards away straight ahead. At the field corner go through a gate and cross a footbridge and stile. Keep along the left-hand edge of a field and then go through a facing gate not far from the dwelling. Keep close to the hedge on the left now and then walk forward along the entrance drive to pass through a gate. Continue along a facing lane and keep straight on at the next junction. Follow the lane over a disused railway track to arrive at the entrance drive of Abbot's Clough Farm, on the right.

FOOD and DRINK

The Wheatsheaf is a large inn serving a wide variety of food and drink, with something to suite every taste. Internally, it has a family area, no-smoking areas and a large indoor play area for children. Children also have an outdoor play area and there is a patio where food and drink can be consumed when the weather is fine (tel: 01928 722986).

PLACES of INTEREST

About 7 miles from Dunham-on-the-Hill via the A56, A5117 and M56 and M53 motorways, is the **Boat Museum** at Ellesmere Port. The museum is set within a historic dock complex and contains the world's largest floating collection of canal craft. There are indoor exhibitions, a shop and a café and boat trips can be arranged (tel: 0151 355 5017).

---

❷ Turn right and follow the farm entrance drive. Pass close to the farmhouse and then keep to the left of a large barn which has brick support piers. Turn right now, to go over a stile at the side of a field gate and after only a further 30 yards, go over a stile and plank-bridge on the left. Climb up a facing slope and then gradually bear left to arrive at a gate at the field corner. Go through the gate and enter a track which follows a line of telegraph poles. The track takes you along level terrain at first and then gradually climbs to a gate before the outbuildings of Lower-hall Farm are reached. Looking across to the right from here there are long views towards Chester, whilst in the middle distance there is a large man-made lake which is used by windsurfers.

Go through the gate and keep to the left of the outbuildings to arrive in front of a facing pond. Turn right here and skirt around the pond to follow a lane which passes close to the farmhouse. Arrive at a facing hairpin bend in a crossing lane. Turn right and descend to a road junction. Turn right, follow the roadside pavement and pass under a bridge.

❸ Leave the road to the left now and go over a stile at the side of a field gate.

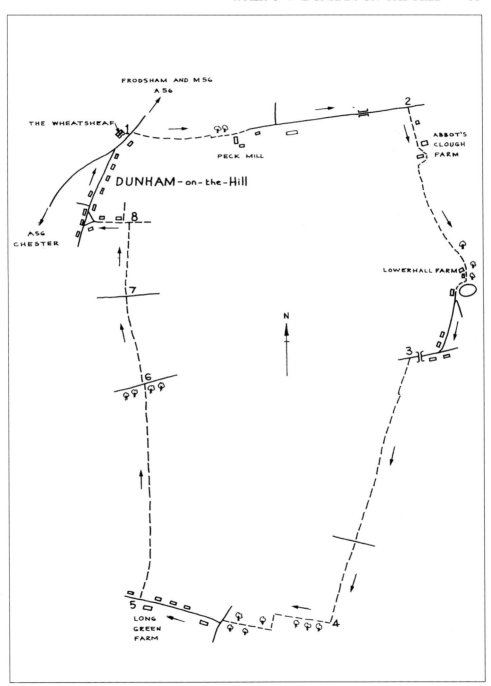

With the stile at your back, walk forward across a rough field aiming about 100 yards to the left of a storage area which can be seen over to the right. Go over a plank-bridge and stile to follow the left-hand edge of the next field. About 90 yards before the end of the field is reached go through a field gate on the left and continue, now with a hedgerow on your immediate right. Where the hedgerow on the right turns away to the right, keep forward, bearing slightly left, to cross the field. Pass over a plank-bridge and stile to enter a very large field. Follow the field edge, keeping a fence on your immediate left. At the field corner go over a fence-stile at the side of a gate and walk straight over a crossing lane. A stile on the opposite side gives access to another large field. Follow the field edge, keeping a hedgerow on your immediate right. On reaching the field corner pass over a stile by the side of a field gate and continue along the edge of the next field, still keeping a hedgerow on your immediate right, to arrive at a plank-bridge and stile on your right just before the end of the field is reached.

❹   Pass over the plank-bridge and stile and follow the edge of the next field keeping trees on your immediate left. On reaching the end of the field go over a stile and cross a plank-bridge through bushes, to emerge into another field. Continue in the same general direction as before and then go through a gate on the left at the field corner. Follow the edge of a large field, keeping a hedgerow and trees on your immediate right. After about 150 yards turn right to follow a rough track between hedges and trees. After ¼ mile, arrive at a crossing lane. Turn left and after only 20 yards, arrive at a junction of lanes. Turn right here, in the direction of Bridge Trafford. In just over ¼ mile, pass Long Green Farm on the left.

❺   Immediately on passing the farm leave the lane to the right, to go over a stile where a footpath sign points towards Dunham. Follow a field edge, keeping a hedgerow on your immediate right and then pass over a stile at the field corner. Gradually bear left across the next field and then go over a stile at the side of a field gate. Follow the edge of the next field to where the hedgerow on the right starts to turn away diagonally to the right. Keep forward now, to shortly pass over a plank-bridge and stile at the right-hand corner of a facing hedgerow. Follow the edge of the next field, keeping a hedgerow on your immediate right and where it turns away to the right keep forward, to arrive at a field gate set between trees.

❻   Go through the gate and walk over a crossing lane diagonally to the left and then pass over a plank-bridge and stile. Keep along the edge of a field where there is a fence on the right and then cross a fence-stile and plank-bridge to enter the next field. Follow the field edge keeping a hedgerow on your immediate right – about 100 yards before the end of the field is reached bear diagonally left to go through a field gap by an old stile and plank-bridge. Bear left now to pass over a stile in a crossing hedgerow – which is about 65 yards to the right of the field corner. Cross a plank-bridge and after a further 80 yards, go over another stile at the side of a field gate.

❼ Walk straight over a crossing lane and through a facing field gate. Follow the field edge, keeping a hedgerow and trees on the immediate left. Go over a stile at the field corner and continue in the same direction as before, to go over another stile which can be seen about 130 yards away at the side of a field gate. Walk straight across the next field, aiming to the right of a garage, which can be seen across the field straight ahead.

❽ Go over a stile to enter a hedged-in track. Turn left and keep on past another track which goes off to the right, pass the front of the garage, and gradually climb between hedgerows. Pass dwellings and arrive close to the village green in the centre of Dunham-on-the-Hill. Turn right past Croft Cottages and follow the roadside pavement. Keep on past a lane which goes off to the left and pass the primary school. The road cuts through the solid sandstone bedrock and descends to join the A56 road close to the Wheatsheaf Inn.

TARVIN

Length : 6 miles

Getting there: Tarvin is 6 miles to the east of Chester at the junction of the A51 and A54.	Parking: There is a free car park in the centre of the village at the side of the George and Dragon Inn.	Map: OS Landranger – Chester (117) (GR 490670).

Tarvin contains an abundance of Georgian buildings constructed in the wake of a disastrous fire in 1752 which destroyed a large number of its former timber-framed cottages. Many of its dwellings are set on visible foundations of solid sandstone rock and the village can boast a fine church which dates back to the 14th century. Tarvin is famous for being the home of the 18th-century penman, John Thomasen, who was also the local schoolmaster. Queen Anne was so impressed with his work that she commissioned him to transcribe the old Greek poets. The school where Thomasen taught is currently a parish hall and cottages adjacent to the church. Opposite the church is a manor house which dates back to the times when the Bishop of Lichfield was Lord of the Manor. Tarvin Hall, which overlooks the broad end of High Street, was rebuilt in brick and conforms to the Georgian style.

Covering a varied and interesting route, the walk takes you through some typical Cheshire countryside on cross-country paths which lead to the tiny villages of Oscroft and Duddon. The return leg of the journey is along minor lanes and tracks which provide a platform for vistas towards the hills of Wales.

THE WALK

❶ From the car park enter Church Street, pass fine Georgian buildings and then turn left, through a gate, to follow a footpath which takes you through the churchyard. Pass through a metal kissing gate at the rear of the church and follow a path along a field edge keeping a fence on the immediate left. The fence turns away to the left but keep forward and then go over a stile in a crossing fence. Keep on, across the next field and go over a bridge which takes you over a stream. Bear diagonally right

---

PLACES of INTEREST

The **Mouldsworth Motor Museum** is 3 miles to the north-east of Tarvin on a minor road which connects Ashton with Mouldsworth. It is a mecca for anyone with an interest in the history of transport. There are examples of early motor cars, Dinky toys, old tools, magazines and signs from a bygone age together with a reconstruction of a 1920s garage which really captures the ambience of an era long since gone (tel: 01928 731781).

---

now, and walk in the direction of farm buildings which can be seen across the field about 550 yards away. About 100 yards before the farm buildings are reached go over a stile on the right. Follow a field edge, keeping a hedgerow on your immediate right, and quickly pass over a stile to enter a hedged-in path. The path takes you between dwellings and emerges onto a crossing road in the village of Oscroft.

❷ Turn right and after only 45 yards leave the road to the left to follow a track which commences at the side of Pump Cottage. Go over a stile at the side of a facing field gate and follow the field edge, keeping a hedgerow on your immediate left. At the field corner turn right and after 45 yards turn left to go over a stile at the side of a field gate. Continue as before, keeping a hedgerow on your immediate left. Pass over a stile at the field corner and continue along the next field edge to where, 15 yards before a copse is reached, you go over a wooden footbridge via a pair of stiles which are set in the hedgerow on your left. Turn right, keeping a hedgerow, and then trees, on your immediate right, to follow the edge of a golf course.

FOOD and DRINK

The Red Lion, thought to have been the first coaching house on the Chester to London route, is a pleasant establishment decorated in a cottage style, although food is not available. The George and Dragon, which was built during the 18th century, has a comfortable bar and serves a selection of home-made dishes using fresh produce. The starters include soup, pâté, prawn cocktail and garlic mushrooms – while a wide choice of main course includes mixed grill, gammon, steak and kidney pie, lasagne, and chilli con carne. A speciality is chicken or beef curry using a recipe known only to the landlady! (tel: 01829 741446).

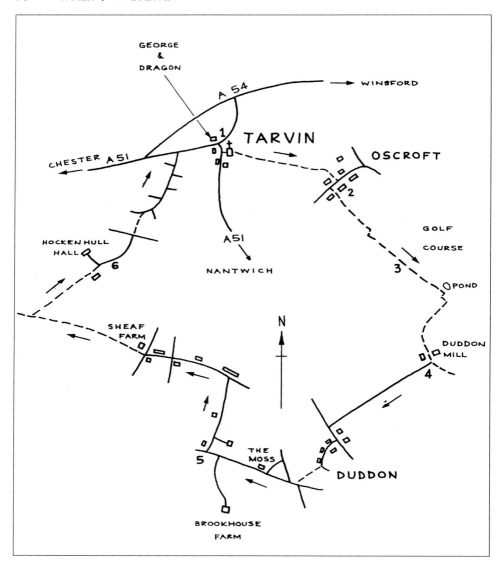

❸ Cross a fairway and continue in the same direction as before, keeping a fence, a ditch and a hedgerow on your immediate right. Over to the left can be seen the golf course club-house. On passing to the right of a small pond go over a stile on the right. Turn left, and then immediately right, to follow the edge of a field, keeping a tall row of conifer trees on your immediate left. Where the conifer trees finish keep forward to follow a track which shortly turns to the left in the direction of a dwelling. Arrive close to the dwelling and turn right and then left to pass close to farm buildings.

The farm is Duddon Mill and, although once used as a mill, the business is now concerned with fruit farming. Immediately on passing a large barn on the right, turn right to follow a narrow lane which leads away from the farm.

❹   Follow the lane for just over ¹/₂ mile to arrive at a crossing road on the outskirts of the village of Duddon. Turn left to follow the roadside pavement and after about 150 yards arrive at a point opposite Burton Lane. Cross the road, taking great care as it is usually quite busy, and enter Burton Lane. Pass an interesting assortment of dwellings. The lane begins to turn to the left but keep forward here to go over a stile into a field. Follow the field edge, keeping trees and hedgerow on your immediate right. A stile at the field corner takes you onto a lane. Turn right. There is a junction of lanes here. Keep forward in the direction of Waverton and Hargrave. Ignore a turn off to the right which goes to Tarvin, pass a couple of dwellings, and keep forward passing another turn off to the right. Again, you are heading in the direction of Waverton and Hargrave. Pass a large farm called The Moss.

❺   Shortly after passing the entrance to Brookhouse Farm turn right to enter Old Moss Lane. Pass Moss Lane Farm and continue, to arrive at a T-junction opposite dwellings. Turn left, past various cottages – including Pilgrim Cottage and Meadow Cottage. After a further 550 yards arrive at a T-junction. Keep forward to go over a stile in a facing hedgerow. A narrow lane takes you past a row of terraced dwellings on your right. Walk straight over a crossing lane

and enter a facing hedged-in track which commences at the side of Sheaf Farm. Follow the track for ¹/₂ mile to arrive at a junction of tracks. Turn sharp right here to proceed along a grassy track where there is a hedgerow on the left and a fence on the right. Shortly, over to the left, the imposing Georgian building of Hockenhull Hall can be seen. Pass a single storey industrial building and arrive at a junction of lanes. The lane to the left goes to Hockenhull Hall but keep forward here to follow a facing lane between banked hedgerows.

❻   Shortly, the tower of Tarvin church comes into view. Go straight over a crossing road, pass through a gate, and keep forward along a macadam lane. Arrive at a crossing road close to houses. Turn right now to follow the roadside pavement. Keep alongside this road passing Heath Close, Heath Drive, Crossfields, Field Lane, Hallfields Road, and Hockenhull Crescent to arrive at a T-junction. Turn right, cross the road, and follow the roadside pavement back into Tarvin village centre.

HIGHER WYCH

Length : 2³/₄ miles

Getting there: From the centre of Malpas, drive south along the B5395 in the direction of Whitchurch and after ³/₄ mile turn right at a signpost to Higher Wych, 2¹/₄ miles away.

Parking: There is limited parking available at the head of the gravel track which leads past the Methodist church – but please ensure that you leave access for local residents.

Map: OS Landranger – Chester (117) (GR 496435).

To the south of Malpas the border between England and Wales is, for about 6 miles, formed by a stream called the Wych Brook. This is a beautiful secluded tract of countryside, little known and where sleepy hamlets nestle in the folds of gentle hills. During years gone by, the waters of the Wych Brook were utilised by

man – which accounts for an abundance of old mills along its banks.

The walk follows a cross-country path which initially climbs away from Higher Wych and then descends into a remote half-hidden valley on the approach to the tiny hamlet of Lower Wych. From Lower Wych a lane leads to a track which is a platform for extensive views across the surrounding countryside. A narrow, fern-lined lane then brings you back to Higher Wych.

THE WALK

❶ Follow the gravel track past the Methodist church and where it finishes go over a facing stile to enter a sloping field. Bear right and climb up the slope. Pass an isolated stile and then go over a stile in a crossing fence. Looking back from here there is a fine view of Higher Wych.

❷ Walk forward, keeping an embankment and trees on the immediate right at first. The path leads to a stile close to the field corner. Cross the stile and gradually climb, keeping a fence and trees about 5 yards away on the right. Pass over the brow of a hill and then gradually descend to proceed along more level terrain. A stile to the left of a field gate takes you onto a crossing track.

❸ Walk straight across the track and pass the corner of a fence which goes off to the right. Descend across a rough pasture then, after 165 yards, cross a dyke via a plank-bridge and stiles. Bear left now and after 45 yards go over a stile in a crossing fence, set between hawthorn bushes, to enter a large rough, sloping field.

FOOD and DRINK

The town of Malpas has a number of inns and eating places. A good choice is the Old Vaults Inn on Church Street, which provides good value bar meals and traditional beers, all served in a pleasing atmosphere (tel: 01948 860245).

PLACES of INTEREST

The country town of **Malpas** is 3 miles by road to the north of Higher Wych. The town has played an important role in the history of the county. The Romans had an encampment here and the Normans built a castle. Although only traces of these early settlements remain, the present-day town contains many interesting buildings and is dominated by a magnificent 14th-century church.

---

❹ The path keeps on generally level terrain and is never too far away from the winding tree-lined Wych Brook on the left. This remote valley abounds with wild-life and there are usually many different species of birds to be seen. After about 1/4 mile, a house comes into view, straight ahead. The path leads to the right of this house. Cross a stile close by the house and follow its entrance drive to arrive at a crossing lane.

❺ Turn left and follow the lane over the Wych Brook (you have now entered Wales). This is the tiny hamlet of Lower Wych. Turn left opposite Brook Farm Cottage to climb along a lane in the direction of Hanmer.

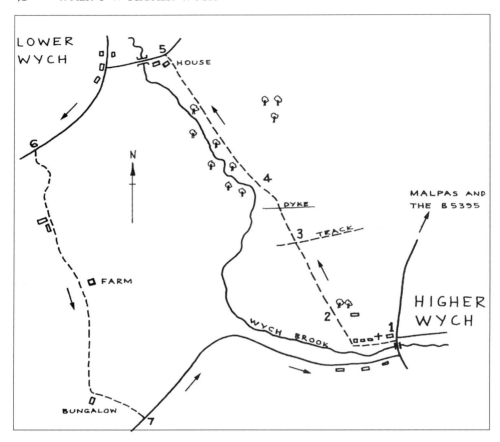

❻ After about 450 yards leave the lane to the left to enter a hedged-in track which descends, turns and climbs. The track is a private road – although pedestrians are allowed to walk along it. Keep on past a dwelling and then continue along more level terrain. Pass a farm, after which there are long views across the surrounding countryside. Follow the track as it turns to the left near a bungalow and then descend to a crossing lane.

❼ Turn left and gradually descend between banks of ferns. A gentle stroll takes you back to Higher Wych and the car.

KELSALL

Length : 4½ miles

Getting there: Kelsall is 9 miles to the east of Chester close to where the A54 Tarvin to Winsford road by-passes the village.	**Parking:** There are parking places in and around the village. Also Th'ouse at Top Inn, which is at the top of the hill on the eastern side of the village, has a large car	park for those visiting the pub. **Map:** OS Landranger – Chester (117) (GR 532686).

Kelsall nestles beneath the sandstone ridge which runs across Cheshire from Helsby to the Peckforton Hills. It is an ancient place, being on the route of an old track which was used by man for many centuries before the Romans improved it to form part of Watling Street – which connected their fort at Chester with Manchester. During more recent times the main road used to pass through the centre of the village; however, life became much quieter when a new bypass was opened which now carries the major flow of traffic to the north of the village. A disastrous fire swept through the village during 1738, hence the majority of the buildings that we see today were built after that date. The village is well known for its mineral springs which have a reputation for promoting good health and longevity. The fertile soil and sheltered location have been used to advantage by local fruit farms and nurseries.

The initial route of the walk is along old lanes which descend to the western side of the village – after which tracks and field paths take you across the Cheshire Plain. A quiet lane leads to the tiny hamlet of Willington Corner. There is then a climb up past the Bronze Age remains of Kelsborrow Castle prior to returning to Kelsall along a minor lane.

THE WALK

❶   From Th'ouse at Top Inn turn left and, on passing the Forester's Arms, bear right to walk along Old Coach Road. Pass a mixture of dwellings and keep on past Hall Lane and Edale Drive. Turn next right to enter Brooms Lane. Pass Longley Avenue and follow the lane as it turns to the left. Arrive at facing dwellings. Duttons Lane goes off to the left here but turn right and descend along a lane which commences at the right-hand side of Hope Cottage. Arrive at Kelsall Methodist church (1884). There is an attractive green in

---

PLACES of INTEREST

The centre of the largest surviving tract of **Delamere Forest** lies about 3 miles to the north-east of Kelsall. There are a number of picnic sites and a display centre – which is located in the now disused Delamere station at Linmere, just over 1 mile north along the B5152 from its intersection with the A556, 2½ miles to the east of Kelsall.

---

front of the church and a memorial gateway. Pass between the church confines and the memorial gateway to join a lane which bears right and then left past Harvey Cottage. Leave the lane to the left now, where a footpath commences at the side of a dwelling called The Mount.

❷   The footpath follows a gully between trees to where, after about 100 yards, there is a junction of paths. Go over a stile on the right here, situated close by a wooden building, and continue along a path where there is a fence on the immediate right. Follow a field edge and go over a stile at the field corner. On the left there are trees and an overgrown hollow-way which is thought to be part of the Roman Watling Street. Follow the next field edge and go over a stile on the left about 90 yards before the end of the field is reached. Descend, cross another stile, and turn left to walk along a lane. Pass Watling Cottage and continue to a crossing road close by the Royal Oak Inn. Cross the road and enter a narrow footpath which commences at the right-hand side of Weldon House. Emerge from the narrow path and walk straight over a crossing track to go over a facing stile into a field.

❸   Walk forward, keeping parallel with a

FOOD and DRINK

Th'ouse at Top Inn is a Greenalls pub where good food and fine ales are served in comfortable surroundings. Apart from a comprehensive set menu there is a daily specials board which extends the available choices – all of which can be consumed in a most attractive beamed dining area (tel: 01829 751784).

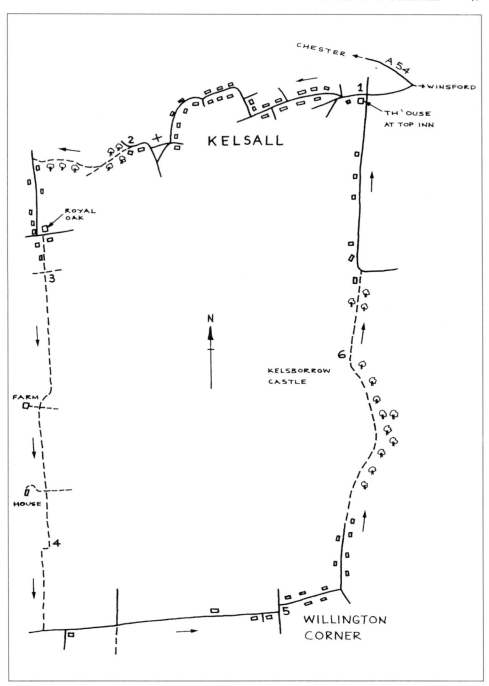

hedgerow on the right about 25 yards away. Go over two stiles in crossing fences which are about 200 yards apart and follow the edge of the next field where there is a fence on the immediate left. On crossing the next stile the path descends to take you through a gate and over a plank-bridge. Bear right now and climb to a stile which can be seen about 65 yards away in a crossing fence. Go over the stile and walk straight over a crossing drive (which leads to a farm on the right). A facing stile gives access to the next field – where there are tall trees on the right. Walk forward, keeping the trees on your right, cross a couple of stiles, and then walk straight over a crossing drive (which leads to a large house on the right). A facing stile gives access to the next field. The path continues along the edge of the next field, with a hedgerow and trees on your immediate right.

❹   Cross a stile at the field corner, turn right, and after only 55 yards turn left, to go over a stile and plank-bridge. The path hugs the edges of the next three fields and leads to a crossing lane via a stile at the side of a field gate. Turn left and follow the lane past Mill Lane and keep on past a lane which goes to Kelsall. A straight length of lane takes you to the hamlet of Willington Corner – where the way is straight ahead to enter Chapel Lane.

❺   Climb past the chapel (now converted into a private dwelling) and arrive at a junction – where the way is left to enter Gooseberry Lane. The lane becomes a track on passing Hillside Cottage. Shortly, to the left of where a concrete drive climbs to a dwelling on the right, there is a footpath. Enter this footpath and ascend the side of the facing hill. On nearing the top of the climb look back to admire extensive views across the Cheshire Plain to the Peckforton Hills.

❻   Go over a stile at the top of the climb and turn right to follow a path which keeps close to a fence on the right. The path becomes a track on crossing the next stile. Go over another stile and climb slightly to where another stile takes you onto a path through trees. Emerge from the trees and pass in front of Lower Fold Cottage to arrive at a crossing lane. Turn left and follow the lane as it turns to the right past the entrance drives of The Weaste and Forest Way. A straight $1/2$ mile takes you back into Kelsall and to Th'ouse at Top Inn.

PECKFORTON

Length : 2¹/₂ miles

Getting there: The A534 runs east to west and connects Nantwich with Farndon. Midway between these two places is the village of Bulkeley. On the western side of the village is an inn called the Bickerton Poacher. Enter Stone House Lane opposite the inn, where signs point to Peckforton and Beeston. Drive down the lane for almost 1¹/₂ miles.

Parking: A ¹/₄ mile after passing tiny Hillside Cottage and a farm, there is a laneside gravel parking area on the left. Park the car here.

Map: OS Landranger – Chester (117) (GR 537561).

Peckforton lies on the eastern side of the sandstone ridge which crosses the Cheshire Plain. Its attractive dwellings fan out along three lanes leading to Beeston, Spurstow and Bulkeley. The area is dominated by two castles, one a medieval ruin, the other a 19th-century building in the style of a grand medieval castle.

The walk follows a path which gently climbs along the flanks of the sandstone ridge – from where there are superb views across the Cheshire Plain. A gentle descent to more level terrain takes you onto cross-country paths, tracks and lanes then into the village, after which a short section of lane leads back to the parking area.

THE WALK

❶ On leaving the parking area, walk along the lane in the direction of Bulkeley to where, after about 150 yards, a footpath crosses the lane. Leave the lane to the right here, to go over a stile where a sign points to Burwardsley and the Sandstone Trail. Climb forward and after 45 yards go over a stile. Gradually climb between widely spaced fences and, after 275 yards, turn right to follow the fence on the right. After a further 165 yards bear left, away from the fence, to follow the line of a grassy ditch which gradually climbs along the hillside. There is shortly a fence, and trees, on your immediate left. A little further on the fence has been replaced by a sturdy stone wall. There are long views to the right from this location across the Cheshire Plain. Two stiles at the field corner lead onto a crossing track.

❷ There is a stone bridge on the immediate left here but turn right to descend along the track. After only 30 yards there is a junction of ways. Keep right here and continue to descend. About 65

FOOD and DRINK

The Bickerton Poacher inn has built up a fine reputation for its food. There is a comprehensive bar meal menu and a daily specials board. Cask conditioned ale is available as well as a wide choice of other drinks. Children are welcome and have their own play area which is situated close to the large car park (tel: 01829 720226).

PLACES of INTEREST

The entrance to **Peckforton Castle** is only $\frac{1}{2}$ mile from the centre of the village (along Stone House Lane in the direction of Beeston). Completed in 1851, it presents a very fine silhouette on the hills above the village and has been used in the making of several historical film dramas. The castle is open daily from early April to early September. You can explore its main building, battlements and perimeter moat walk – but it should be noted that the surrounding lands are not under the ownership of the castle.

---

yards further on, and shortly after passing a metal gate, there is another junction. Turn left here, to enter a gravel track, but, after only 15 yards, turn right to follow a footpath along the edge of a wood. After 90 yards cross a stile to emerge from the trees. Descend across a sloping field to go over another stile and then turn right to continue with a fence on your immediate right. About 100 yards further on another stile gives access to a large undulating field. A well-defined path takes you to a crossing lane via a pair of stiles.

❸ Turn left along the lane. After 165 yards leave the lane to the right over a double stile. Two paths commence at this point. Keep forward here across the facing field in the direction of Peckforton Hall Lane (ignore the path to the left which goes to Beeston Moss and Bunbury). Having crossed the field, the way is forward through a gap, but turn around here to admire a fine view of the twin castles of Peckforton and Beeston. Go through the gap and bear slightly right to cross the next field. On reaching the far side of the field go over a stile to join a crossing track.

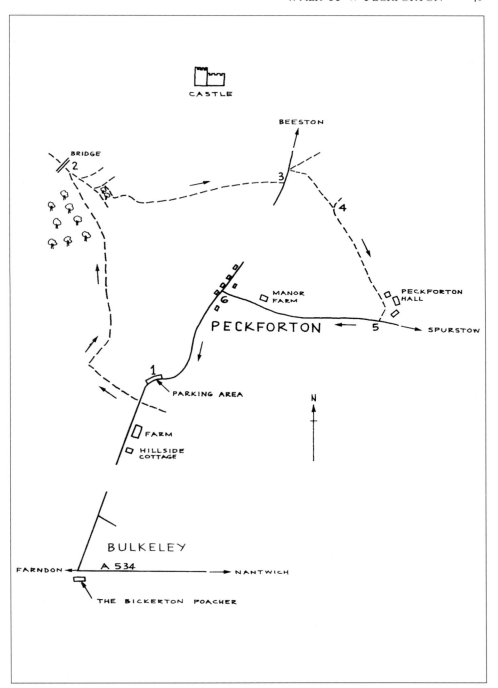

❹   Turn right and follow the track, which quickly bends to the left. Gradually climb along the track. The track continues along more level terrain and takes you to a facing double gate. Immediately on passing through the gate keep to the left, by a hedgerow, and then turn right, where the path stays close to a fence. On the left there are large buildings. The path joins the entrance drive of Peckforton Hall, which leads to a crossing lane.

❺   Turn right along the lane. After ¼ mile pass Manor Farm and continue, to arrive at a junction of lanes in the village of Peckforton. Take time to look around.

Many of the houses have distinctive cast-iron, diamond-paned windows and large chimneys. All the village houses were originally thatched, however only two remain – the others having been re-roofed with slates or clay tiles. In the garden of one of the cottages along the lane to the right there is a sculpture of an elephant and castle which was carved around 1859 by a local stonemason.

❻   Retrace your steps back to the head of the lane by which you entered the village and walk past it – in the direction of Bulkeley. A gentle stroll leads back to the parking area, which is a little over ¼ mile away.

A village cottage complete with elephant and castle!

TIVERTON

Length : 5 miles

Getting there: Tiverton village is ¼ mile to the west of the A49, less than 2 miles south of Tarporley.	**Parking:** There is a lay-by at either side of the head of the lane which connects the A49 with the village.	**Map:** OS Landranger – Chester (117) (GR 553603).

Almost in the shadow of the huge rock which is topped by the ruins of Beeston Castle, Tiverton enjoys an enviable location. There are attractive dwellings, a village green, and views to rival any in the county. Close by are the waters of the Shropshire Union Canal which adds a further interesting flavour to the area.

The walk initially follows a lane which takes you away from the village and to a cross-country path, for a gradual descent across fields to the Shropshire Union Canal. A waterside path then follows the course of the canal to Bunbury Locks, after which a mixture of lanes and paths lead back to Tiverton.

THE WALK

❶ On leaving the car there is a choice of two routes into the village. The first is to follow the lane where a sign tells you that Tiverton is $^1/_4$ mile away, to arrive in the centre of the village.

The second is to walk to the top end of the lay-by on the right-hand side of the lane and enter a narrow fenced-in path at Cedar Bank – where a footpath sign points to Tiverton. The path takes you between dwellings, through a gate, and then close to a sports field on the right. Pass through another gate. The path becomes a grassy track between hedgerows. After passing through an old gateway there are hedges and trees on both sides. On meeting a junction turn left to shortly arrive in the centre of the village.

The village green is surrounded by interesting cottages and the rather plain building of the Primitive Methodist church, constructed in 1864. In the centre of the village green is the war memorial.

❷   Follow a laneside pavement away from the village green to pass a dwelling on the left called Chester's Corner. Continue past the Old Post Office Cottage and keep on past The Dale and Grove House. Leave the dwellings behind and continue along the lane to where, about $^1/_4$ mile further on, there is a junction close by Tiverton Hall.

FOOD and DRINK

A little over halfway around the walk the route takes you past the Traveller's Rest Inn, where liquid refreshment can be obtained. If a meal is required, a good choice is the Red Fox, which is a country inn and eating house situated a little over $^1/_2$ mile to the north of Tiverton at the junction of the A49, A51 and B5152 roads (tel: 01829 733152).

PLACES of INTEREST

Beeston Castle is reached along a minor road which joins the A49 about $^1/_2$ mile to the south of the parking location for the walk. Built during the early 13th century, the castle played an important role during the Civil War (1642-49). Although now ruinous, the site is an interesting one, and the views from the summit of the crag on which the castle stands are superb.

---

❸   Turn left to enter a hedged-in track where a sign points to Beeston Brook. After only 55 yards follow the track as it turns to the left and pass close to a dwelling. Pass over a plank-bridge and stile at the side of a field gate and walk forward down the middle of a large field. Go over a stile in a crossing fence to enter a sloping field. Bear right now, and descend, to go over another stile about 55 yards away. Walk forward and then bear left to cross a rough undulating field, where the canal can be seen about 90 yards away over to the right. The path very gradually converges with the canal, and when the end of the field is reached, there is a stile which is only about 10 yards away from the canal. Go over the stile and follow the edge of the next field, keeping close to the canal. A short length of track then takes you to a crossing road. Turn right, cross the Shropshire Union Canal, and then descend onto the towpath.

❹   Turn right and pass under the bridge you have just walked across (No 107). Keep on past a couple of locks and, about 1 mile after joining the canal towpath, arrive at a bridge (106) which carries a lane over the canal. This is the tiny hamlet of Tilstone Bank, where there are interesting waterside dwellings with attractive gardens. Keep on,

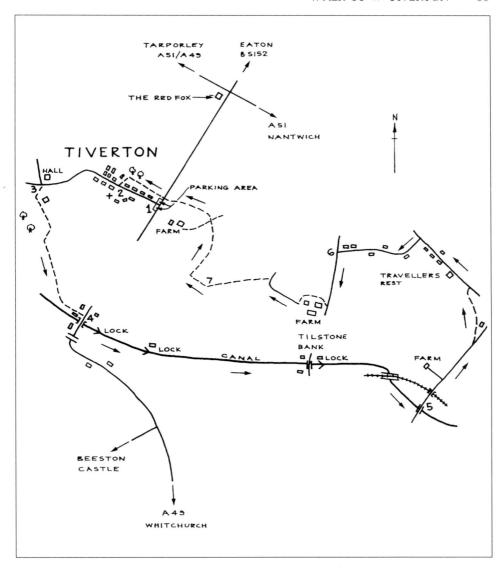

TARPORLEY
A51/A49

EATON
B 5152

THE RED FOX

A51
NANTWICH

N

TIVERTON

HALL

PARKING AREA

FARM

3

1

2

FARM

7

6

TRAVELLERS
REST

4

LOCK

LOCK

CANAL

FARM

TILSTONE
BANK

LOCK

FARM

5

BEESTON
CASTLE

A49
WHITCHURCH

along the towpath, pass another lock and then, about ¹/₂ mile further on, pass under a bridge which carries a railway line over the canal. Leave the towpath to the right of the next bridge, just before Bunbury Locks are reached.

❺ Turn left and follow Bowes Gate Road over the canal. Cross the railway and keep on past a farm entrance drive. Enter a hedged-in grassy track on the left shortly, just before a bungalow is reached. Follow the track to a crossing road, then turn left to follow the roadside pavement. The route takes you past the Traveller's Rest Inn, where liquid refreshment can be obtained. Keep on past the delightful Grove Cottage, then pass The Firs, The Gables and Barn Lodge, to enter a narrow lane which goes off to the left. A sign at the head of this lane says: 'Unsuitable for heavy goods vehicles'. The lane bends, passes dwellings and leads, after about ¹/₂ mile, to a junction of lanes.

❻ Turn left along a lane to where, after ¹/₄ mile, you arrive at farm outbuildings on the right. Go over a stile at the side of a gate and follow a sandy track on the right here. The track skirts around the edge of the farm outbuildings and leads to a stile at the rear – the crossing of which takes you onto a concrete drive. Turn right and follow the drive away from the farm. After about 200 yards the drive turns to the right. Go over a stile on the left here to enter a large field. There is a fence on the right now, but the path gradually bears left, away from the fence, and takes you to

a stile in a crossing fence to the left of hawthorn bushes. There is a fine view of the twin castles of Peckforton and Beeston from this path.

❼ Cross the stile and follow the edge of the next field, keeping a fence on your immediate left. After about 100 yards, arrive at the field corner, turn right and continue, with a hedgerow now on your immediate left. After 165 yards, follow the hedgerow as it bends to the left and then go through a facing gate. Immediately on passing through the gate keep forward, across a field, to go over a pair of stiles which take you over a crossing track (the track goes to a farm and outbuildings which can be seen over to the left). Having crossed the stiles, follow the edge of the next field, keeping a hedgerow on your immediate right. Go over a stile and descend steps to arrive at a crossing road.

Cross the road, taking care, and arrive back at the parking area near the head of the lane which goes to Tiverton.

Canal side scene near Beeston

MARBURY

Length : 6 miles

| **Getting there:** Marbury is 3 miles to the north of Whitchurch and 2 miles to the east of the A49 Whitchurch to Tarporley road. | **Parking:** There are parking places in and around the village. If you are visiting the village inn, the Swan, then you may use its car park. | **Map:** OS Landranger – Chester (117) (GR 561457). |

The tiny picturesque village of Marbury is tucked away in a quiet green corner of Cheshire, close to the Shropshire border. The village lies between two meres and its lovely old church rests on a gentle hillside overlooking the larger mere. To the north of the village is the Shropshire Union Canal, where the pleasure craft of today have taken the place of working boats of yesteryear. At the centre of the village is the green, where a circular seat encircles an oak tree planted to commemorate the Battle of Waterloo. The village inn, the Swan, overlooks the green as does a row of old cottages at the side of which is a lane which leads to the church. Records show that a church existed on this site in 1299, although the present building dates from the 15th century. There are many interesting stone carvings around the outside and the church contains an original pulpit which is still in use.

From Marbury, the walk takes you across fields to the Shropshire Union Canal. The route then follows the canal towpath to Willey Moor Lock before a gentle climb to Wirswall, where there are lovely panoramic views over the lush Cheshire countryside. The return to Marbury takes in a path along the edge of Marbury Mere.

THE WALK

❶ From the village green, pass in front of the Swan in the direction of Marley Green and Wrenbury and continue past a mixture of dwellings. On passing a large walled house on the left – which is the last house in the village – go through a metal kissing gate on the left. Climb along the edge of a field keeping a hedgerow on your immediate right and then go over a stile at the field corner. Bear left now and, keeping a hedgerow on your immediate left, gently climb along a field edge. After about 100 yards, bear diagonally right and cross the

---

FOOD and DRINK

The Swan is an excellent choice for a meal or leisurely drink. There is a wide choice of home-made food with various main meals, starters, sweets, light snacks and sandwiches – all served in a most attractive lounge bar. A daily specials board extends the choice of food even further. Meals are served every lunchtime, except Monday, and every evening (tel: 01948 663715). Halfway around the walk and next to the Shropshire Union Canal is the Willey Moor Lock Tavern where food and drink can be taken in a pleasant waterside location (tel: 01948 663274).

PLACES of INTEREST

About 5 miles to the north of Marbury, and just off the A49, are the park and gardens of **Cholmondeley Castle Estate**. They are open on Sunday and bank holiday afternoons during April, and on Wednesday, Thursday, Sunday and bank holiday afternoons between May and the beginning of October. For information telephone: 01829 720383.

---

field corner to go over a stile in a crossing hedgerow. Walk forward and gradually descend across a large undulating field, aiming to the right of a dwelling which can be seen about 400 yards away. Pass through a gate and then bear left to converge with a track. A metal kissing gate at the side of a field gate gives access to a lane, where the way is right. Go over a stone bridge and then cross the Shropshire Union Canal. There is a lock here and adjacent cottage. Go through a gate on the left and walk past the lock to follow the canal towpath.

❷ Follow the canal towpath and after $1/2$ mile pass under a bridge. About 1 mile further on, pass under bridge 25 which carries the A49 over the canal. Keep on past Quoisley Lock and after a further $3/4$ mile arrive at Willey Moor Lock.

There is a waterside pub here, called the Willey Moor Lock Tavern, where food and drink can be purchased. Leave the canal at this point, where a fence-stile and plank-bridge give access to a field on the opposite side of the canal.

❸ Keep along the edge of the field – there is a hedgerow on the immediate left here. A stile at the side of a gate takes you onto a track. Cross a stile at the field corner

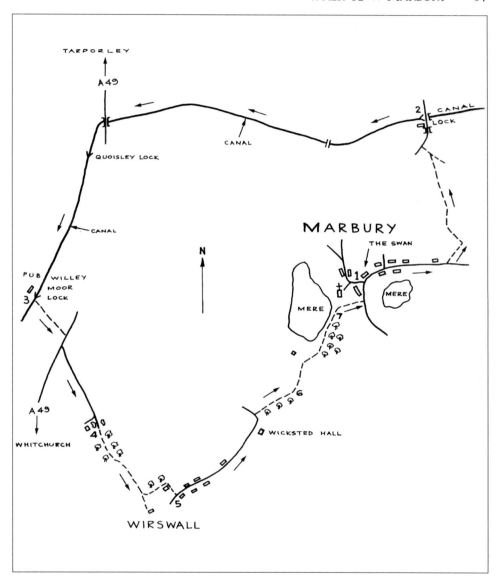

to arrive at a road. Turn right and then immediately left to enter Bradeley Green Lane. Gradually climb along the lane. The lane finishes close to a dwelling where there are ponds but keep forward here to enter a facing hedged-in grassy track.

❹ Gradually climb along the track and in about ¹/₂ mile, just before level terrain is reached, outbuildings can be seen about 200 yards straight ahead. There is a junction of tracks here. Go through a gate on the left and follow a hedged-in track which shortly takes you past a dwelling. Turn sharp right now and pass the dwelling, to arrive at a crossing lane in the hamlet of Wirswall.

❺ Turn left and follow the lane past a mixture of dwellings, including Rose Cottage and Swallow Rise, to where, on passing the entrance of Wicksted Hall, the lane turns sharply to the left. There are two footpaths here, which are only 15 yards apart. Take the right-hand path – which commences over a stile at the side of a field gate. If the day is clear, stop for a few moments to admire the view. Straight ahead, in the near distance, can be seen the village of Marbury with its church overlooking the mere. On the skyline, diagonally to the left, are the Peckforton Hills – whilst in the middle distance Quoisley Mere can be seen.

Follow the field edge, keeping a hawthorn hedge on your immediate right. After 165 yards, the hedge on the right finishes, but go over a stile here to enter a large undulating field.

❻ Descend across the field, bearing slightly right, to a stile which is about 275 yards away in a crossing hedge. On crossing the stile a well-defined path leads across the next field. Go over a stile at the side of a field gate to enter a rough pasture. Follow generally level terrain now, where a dwelling can be seen half–hidden by trees on a rise on the left, then go over a stile close to trees. The footpath hugs the edge of the trees. A stile at the side of a field gate takes you onto a path which follows the edge of Marbury Mere.

❼ Where the trees on the immediate right finish, go over a stile to continue along the water's edge. On crossing the next stile bear right to leave the waterside and cross a field to go through a small gate at the side of a field gate which gives access to a lane. Turn left and follow the lane back into Marbury village.

The Swan Inn overlooks the village green

ANTROBUS

Length : 3 miles

Getting there: The A559 runs in a south-easterly direction from junction 10 of the M56 motorway to Lostock Gralam, near Northwich. About 2 miles along this road from the M56	there is an inn called the Antrobus Arms. **Parking:** There is parking available in and around the village. Visitors to the Antrobus Arms may park in	their car park. **Maps:** OS Landranger – Manchester (109) and Stoke-on-Trent (118) (GR 636796).

The village is the only one so called in England and people named Antrobus take their name from it. Its dwellings are a mixture of the old and the new, with some of the older cottages being of cruck construction. There is a church, post office, village hall and a small green. The village is thought to have been on the course of a Roman road linking it with the old salt town of Northwich (Condate).

The walk commences at the Antrobus Arms; follows lanes and tracks to Antrobus Methodist church, after which cross-country paths lead to the village. A section of lane walking is followed by a path bringing you back to the lane which leads to the inn.

THE WALK

❶ On leaving the inn turn left to enter Meg Lane, which commences opposite Wheatsheaf Lane. After ¼ mile, arrive at a junction. Turn left here, along Knutsford Road and after 400 yards arrive at another junction. Turn right to enter Reed Lane and keep on past a narrow lane which goes off to the left. Pass Ashwood Brow Farm and The Old Pump House. About ¼ mile further on, the lane turns sharply to the left at Peel Hall.

❷ Enter a facing track here, where a sign indicates Antrobus Hall. An obvious track takes you between farm outbuildings and then a straight length of track between hedgerows leads to a crossing lane. Turn right and arrive in front of the plain building of Antrobus Methodist church.

❸ Enter the church confines through a double gate and pass to the right of the church building. Go over a facing stile which is set in a fence surrounding the churchyard. Walk forward across a field and then go over a fence-stile at the side of a facing field gate. Keep on, across the next field, in the same general direction as

---

PLACES of INTEREST

Arley Hall and Gardens are about 3 miles by road to the north-east of Antrobus. The Hall is a fine example of early Victorian 'Jacobean' style and is surrounded by 12 acres of beautiful gardens. Apart from the Hall and gardens there is a chapel and a gift shop, and a restaurant sited in a former Tudor barn. The gardens are normally open during the afternoon between April and September (closed on Mondays) but the opening times for the Hall vary (tel: 01565 777353).

---

before, to go over a stile at the left-hand side of facing trees. Turn right now, along a field edge, keeping a hedgerow and trees on your immediate right. Turn left at the field corner and continue. On reaching the end of the field turn left and, after only 10 yards, go over a double stile and plank-bridge on the right. Follow the edge of the next field, keeping a hedgerow on your immediate left. At the field corner there is a junction of paths. Turn right here, to follow a hedged-in path. The path becomes a hedged-in track and leads to a crossing lane.

❹ Turn right along the lane and pass Keepers Cottage. Keep on past a lane which goes off to the right. About 45 yards further on, there is a fenced-in track on the left. To the left of this track there is a small wooden gate. Go through the gate and walk forward, keeping a fence on the right about 3 yards away, to follow the edge of a large field. Where the fence on the right bends away to the right, keep forward in the same direction as before to gradually descend to a stile which can be seen in a crossing hedge straight ahead. Cross the stile, go over a plank-bridge, and

---

FOOD and DRINK

Previously a coaching inn, the Antrobus Arms is over 200 years old and has been extensively modernised during recent years to good effect. It was formerly known as the Wheatsheaf. The inn serves bar food every lunchtime and during the evening. The menu is varied and constantly changing; an appetising 'baguette' menu is also available which offers numerous tasty fillings to choose from. There is a patio, and an outside play area for children (tel: 01606 891333).

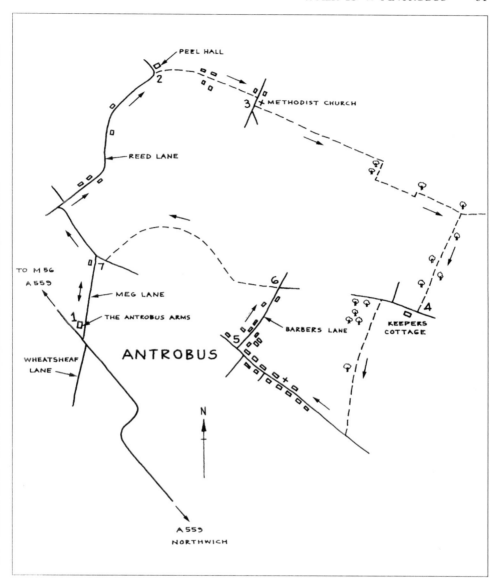

PEEL HALL

MMETHODIST CHURCH

REED LANE

TO M 56
A 559

MEG LANE

THE ANTROBUS ARMS

WHEATSHEAF
LANE

ANTROBUS

BARBERS LANE

KEEPERS
COTTAGE

N

A 559
NORTHWICH

follow the left-hand edge of the next field in the same general direction as before. Pass over a stile at the field corner and turn right to walk along a roadside pavement which takes you into the village of Antrobus.

Close to the junction in the centre of the village is the combined post office and general store – opposite which is a small green where there is a seat to rest on. A short distance along School Lane is the village hall and school.

❺ Leave the village along Barbers Lane and keep on past modern dwellings. A little further on, there is a delightful black and white house on the left and the picturesque Barbers Lane Cottage on the right. Arrive at Keepers Lane, which goes off to the right.

❻ Turn left now, to go over a stile which takes you into a field. Follow the field edge, keeping a hedgerow and ditch on your immediate left. Go over a stile close to where a hedgerow juts out onto the field edge. Follow the edge of the next two fields, keeping a hedgerow on your immediate right and pass over two stiles. Follow the edge of the next field, which shortly turns to the left and go over a stile on reaching the field corner.

❼ Turn right along Knutsford Road and then turn next left to enter Meg Lane. You are now back on part of your initial route. Follow Meg Lane back to the Antrobus Arms and your car.

Cottage in the village

WHITEGATE

Length : 4¹/₂ miles

Getting there: Whitegate Way Station, just over 1 mile to the south-west of Whitegate village, is the major access point onto Whitegate Way and is situated between the A556 and A54 roads, 3 miles to the north-west of Winsford. From Winsford, leave the A54 at Salterswall and continue in the direction of Sandiway. Fork left at Martonsands and then turn next left. From the A556 at Sandiway take a minor road in the direction of Whitegate and Winsford and in almost 2 miles turn second right and then keep straight on at the next junction.

Parking: At the Whitegate Way Station car park and picnic site.

Map: OS Landranger – Stoke-on-Trent (118) (GR 616680).

At the very centre of the county, Whitegate is an attractive village of thatched cottages and well-kept dwellings. The village takes its name from a large white gate which stood opposite the church at the entrance to Vale Royal Park – once the setting of one of the finest and largest Cistercian abbeys in England. When the annual summer fete is held, the village green is awash with colour as maypole dancers weave intricate patterns with their multi-coloured ribbons.

From the picnic area at Whitegate Way Station, the walk takes you through the sleepy hamlet of Foxwist Green and then across fields to the village of Whitegate. From Whitegate, quiet country lanes lead to Whitegate Way for a gentle stroll of 1$\frac{1}{2}$ miles along a picturesque section of the former railway line.

THE WALK

❶ From the parking area walk to the rear of the large sign of 'Whitegate', which once identified the railway station, and follow the course of the now redundant railway in the direction of Birchwood and Sandiway. Pass under a bridge which has had extra wooden support beams added and leave Whitegate Way to the right – where a permissive path leads to a road. Turn left and follow the roadside verge to where, after about 165 yards, there is a junction. Turn right here, in the direction of Winsford. Pass the entrances to large detached dwellings and then turn next left by Cassia Green Farm. At the next junction keep forward to enter Beauty Bank and shortly arrive at the Plough Inn.

FOOD and DRINK

Just over $\frac{1}{2}$ mile into the walk the route takes you past the Plough Inn – which is situated at Beauty Bank, Foxwist Green, close to the Methodist chapel. The Plough, which was once a small cottage, has been developed into an attractive establishment where ramblers are made welcome. A Robinson's house, the inn provides a wide range of home-made lunches, served seven days a week (tel: 01606 889455).

PLACES of INTEREST

About 4 miles by road to the north-east of Whitegate village is the town of **Northwich** – where Britain's only **Salt Museum** relates the fascinating story of Cheshire's oldest industry. The route is signposted from the A556 and from Northwich town centre. The Salt Museum is open every day except Monday: Tuesday to Friday 10 am to 5 pm and at weekends 2 pm to 5 pm (tel: 01606 41331).

---

❷ From the Plough continue past the Methodist church and then turn left about 165 yards further on to follow a track between dwellings. (This track begins to the left of dwelling No 43.) Go through a facing field gate and follow a grassy track, keeping a hedgerow on your immediate left. At the end of the field pass over a stile at the side of a gate and descend across the next field to a stile which can be seen about 65 yards away. On crossing the stile the path descends more steeply. Go over a plank-bridge and stile and then climb along the edge of the next field, keeping a fence and hedgerow on your immediate right. After about 90 yards, go over a stile set in the hedgerow on your right, and continue in the same direction as before, but now with the hedgerow on your immediate left. On reaching the end of the field pass over a stile to enter a lane.

❸ Turn right along the lane. After about 200 yards a lane joins from the left, immediately followed by the entrance to a dwelling called Swallow's Nest. Go over a stile about 5 yards to the right of this entrance to enter a field. Follow a path which stays close by the garden hedgerow of Swallow's Nest and then go over a stile at

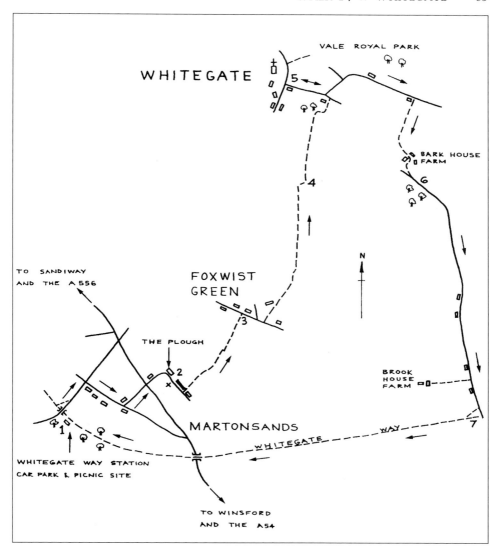

WHITEGATE

VALE ROYAL PARK

5

BARK HOUSE
FARM

4

6

TO SANDIWAY
AND THE A556

FOXWIST
GREEN

N

3

THE PLOUGH

2

BROOK
HOUSE
FARM

MARTONSANDS

WHITEGATE   WAY   7

WHITEGATE

1

WHITEGATE WAY STATION
CAR PARK & PICNIC SITE

TO WINSFORD
AND THE A54

the field corner. Keep a fence and hedgerow on the immediate right now and, after only 45 yards, go over a stile set between holly bushes to enter a large field. The path follows the left-hand edge of the field, where there is a hedgerow and trees on the immediate left. Pass through a field gap and continue along the edge of the next field.

Turn right at the field corner to arrive, after only a further 45 yards, at a field gap on the left.

❹   Go through the gap and follow a well-defined path which gradually descends across a large undulating field, from where the houses of the village of Whitegate can be seen amongst trees straight ahead. On reaching the trees go through a gap in a fence, then turn right to cross a wooden footbridge. Turn right, and then left, to follow a path which skirts around the edge of a garden, and then climb up steps. Go through a gate and turn left at a junction of lanes to follow Grange Lane, which takes you into the village of Whitegate.

Straight ahead is the school building, whilst over to the right stands the church of St Mary. There has been a church on this site since medieval times, but the present building dates from 1875. Between the church and the school building is the village green, where maypole dancing still takes place.

❺   Having surveyed the village, re-enter Grange Lane, then bear left and climb along Mill Lane. Pass Sutton Field and follow Mill Lane as it bears to the right. Keep on past a row of dwellings on the left and, 275 yards further on, arrive at the entrance driveway of Bark House Farm. Follow the hedged-in driveway to arrive close by the large three-storey farmhouse. Turn right here to enter a gravel track which takes you past the front of the house. The track turns to the left and descends to a lane.

❻   Turn left along the lane. Follow this quiet pleasant undulating lane for over $^{1}/_{2}$ mile, passing a mixture of dwellings and the entrance drive of Brook House Farm en route. Shortly after passing the farm entrance drive join the Whitegate Way to the right of where a bridge once carried the railway over the lane.

❼   Whitegate Way follows the route of a railway which was built in the 1880s to transport salt from the mines at Winsford up to a junction with the Manchester to Chester line. Follow this picturesque linear walk for $1^{1}/_{2}$ miles, to arrive back at Whitegate Way Station.

ACTON

Length : 4 miles

Getting there: Acton straddles the A534 Nantwich to Wrexham road a little over 1 mile to the west of Nantwich.	**Parking:** There is a large free car park in the centre of the village, virtually opposite the Star Inn.	**Map:** OS Landranger – Stoke-on-Trent (118) (GR 632531).

The approach to Acton is dominated by the 800 year old tower of St Mary's church – around which the final stages of the Civil War battle of Nantwich were fought in 1644. Originally established by monks from Combermere Abbey in 1180, the church contains 14th and 17th-century effigies as well as elaborate wooden carvings. The graveyard contains the tomb of Albert Hornby – who was the England cricket captain during the 1882 Test Match against Australia which gave birth to The Ashes. There is a village pub, the Star Inn, and a number of delightful cottages.

The walk initially follows the course of an ancient track before joining a lane which leads to the towpath of the Llangollen branch of the Shropshire Union

Canal. A pleasant stretch of waterside path is followed by a scenic cross-country path which brings you back to the village.

THE WALK

❶ On leaving the car park cross the road and turn left to pass in front of the Star Inn. Immediately on passing the inn bear right to follow a track where a sign points towards Marsh Lane. Pass a dwelling and keep forward along the facing track. Stay on the main track and pass close to a farm. Go through a gate – after which the track is hedged-in. Emerge from the track at a junction of lanes, where there are dwellings on left and right.

❷ Follow the lane which goes to the right. Keep on past a farm and arrive at crossroads. The way is forward here to enter a straight section of lane. After ¼ mile, arrive at crossroads. Keep forward now to enter the hamlet of Stoneley Green (the lane is headed by a no-through-road sign, but this only applies to vehicles).

❸ On passing the black and white End

PLACES of INTEREST

Lying just off the A534 between Acton and Nantwich is magnificent **Dorfold Hall**. The Jacobean exterior has survived the ravages of time and the interior is also in a fine state of repair. The Hall is set amidst attractive gardens which are a delight during the summer months. The Hall and gardens are open on Tuesdays and bank holiday Mondays – April to October, between 2 pm and 5 pm. Just over 1 mile to the east of Acton along the A534 is the fine old market town of **Nantwich**, famous for its half-timbered buildings and beautiful church.

Cottage the lane becomes a hedged-in track which turns sharply to the right. Follow the track as it turns to the right and then go through a gate to enter a large field. Walk forward, keeping a hedgerow on your immediate left, and after about 90 yards go through a gate on the left. A grassy track leads to a bridge which can be seen about 165 yards away.

❹ Do not cross the bridge but go over a fence-stile at its right-hand side to join the towpath of the Llangollen branch of the Shropshire Union Canal. Turn right and walk along beside the canal, an endless source of fascination with its boats and wildlife. Pass an isolated lock and walk under bridge 9. At the next bridge (8) leave the canal and go to the right to arrive at a junction of roads.

❺ The road to the right goes to Stoneley Green and Ravensmoor, but keep diagonally left to follow a road which goes to Acton and Nantwich. Immediately pass the semi-detached Swanley Cottages and after 130 yards leave the road to the right, to enter a rough driveway where there is a

---

FOOD and DRINK

The attractive timber-framed Star Inn is reputed to date from 1590. Its earlier name was the 'Stirrup Cup' and its association with horse-mounted customers is emphasised by the stone mounting-block close by the front entrance. The inn has a pleasant bar and an attractive cosy lounge on two levels where a range of bar meals, snacks, sandwiches, salads and sweets are served. During wintertime two fires provide a warming glow and when the weather is fine outside benches can be utilised. Families are assured of a friendly welcome from the landlord and his wife (tel: 01270 627296).

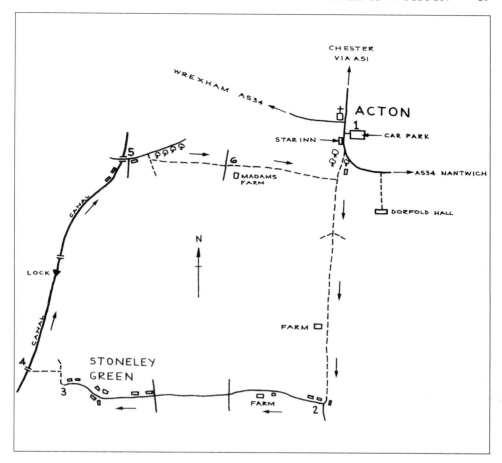

hedgerow on the right and trees on the left. After only 65 yards, the trees on the left finish. Leave the driveway to the left here, to follow a well-defined path which bears diagonally right across a field. Pass through a gap in a crossing hedgerow and continue across the next field. Arrive at a crossing lane opposite the entrance drive to Madam's Farm.

❻   Enter the farm approach drive – but leave it after only about 90 yards through a

gap on the left at the side of silver birch trees. Turn right now, keeping a hedge and fence on your immediate right, at first, to follow the edge of a field. Where the hedge on the right turns away to the right keep forward to follow a well-defined path across a large undulating field. Pass through a gap in a crossing hedgerow – there is a splendid view of Acton church across the fields to the left here. The path leads to a crossing track – where your way is left. You are now back on part of your initial route. A short stroll takes you back into Acton.

CHURCH MINSHULL

Length : 7 miles

Getting there: The B5074 connects Winsford with Nantwich. Church Minshull straddles this road midway between the two places.

Parking: There is a parking area at the side of the Badger Inn and adjacent post office (for patrons of the inn).

Map: OS Landranger – Stoke-on-Trent (118) (GR 666607).

Church Minshull is a typically 17th-century Cheshire village which is rich in half-timbered dwellings. It is thought that the village evolved due to its situation at the point where a spur of the Roman road from Nantwich to Middlewich crossed the river Weaver. At the centre of the village is St Bartholomew's church, completed in 1702 on the site of two previous churches.

Opposite the Badger Inn is Church Farm, whose porch juts out towards the road and is supported on pillars. The farm was the home of Elizabeth Minshull before she became the third wife of the poet John Milton in 1660. The village has a smithy and a mill – which, apart from grinding corn, provided electricity for the whole community up to 1960.

The first half of the walk has a watery content as it takes you along the towpath of a section of the Middlewich branch of the Shropshire Union Canal and then along field paths to cross the river Weaver. The return leg takes in a typical Cheshire lane before returning to Church Minshull along field paths and tracks.

THE WALK

❶ Pass in front of the Badger Inn and walk past the church of St Bartholomew. Turn right now to enter Cross Lane. Follow the lane over the infant river Weaver and climb to a bridge over the Shropshire Union Canal. Do not cross the bridge but go over a stile on the left and descend onto the canal towpath. Turn left and follow the towpath away from the bridge – bridge 14. The canal is the Middlewich branch of the Shropshire Union Canal, which was once extensively used for transporting coal and salt.

Follow the towpath for over 1 mile and pass under bridges 15, 16 and 18. On the left shortly there is a now defunct stable block and isolated dwelling. Immediately on passing under bridge 19 leave the canal to the left and climb to pass through a small wooden gate.

FOOD and DRINK

As with many Cheshire inns, the Badger was originally a farmhouse and is today a Grade II listed building of historic and architectural interest. The inn has built up a good reputation for its food and patrons have the option of using the restaurant or choosing a bar meal; all the beers are served from the cask. There is an attractive beer garden at the rear. (tel: 01270 522607) At the side of the inn there is a post office and store where sandwiches and pies can be purchased.

PLACES of INTEREST

Less than 6 miles to the south of Church Minshull, and accessible via the B5074 and A51 roads, is the old market town of **Nantwich**, famous for its fine half-timbered buildings and beautiful church.

---

❷ Do not walk over bridge 19 but go over a stile at the side of a field gate and bear right to cross a rough pasture. After 165 yards go over a stile at the right-hand side of trees. The path leads to a stile in a crossing hedgerow which can be seen about 100 yards away. Cross the stile and bear right to proceed in the direction of trees which can be seen about 220 yards away. Bear right on reaching the trees keeping a hedgerow, and the trees, on your immediate left. Pass over a stile and continue along the edge of the trees. Descend now and then go over a stile at the field corner, at the side of a gate. Keep along the edge of the next field where the river Weaver can be seen through trees on the left and arrive at a sturdy footbridge which traverses the river.

❸ Cross the river and then pass to the right of a facing gate to climb up a rough grassy slope. At the top of the climb go over a stile at the side of a tree. Turn right here, to follow a hedged-in track. The track becomes a macadam lane and takes you past various dwellings. On passing a site for mobile homes arrive at a crossing road. Turn right and follow the roadside verge for 220 yards and then turn left opposite the ornate entrance gates of Ashbrook Towers to enter Paradise Lane.

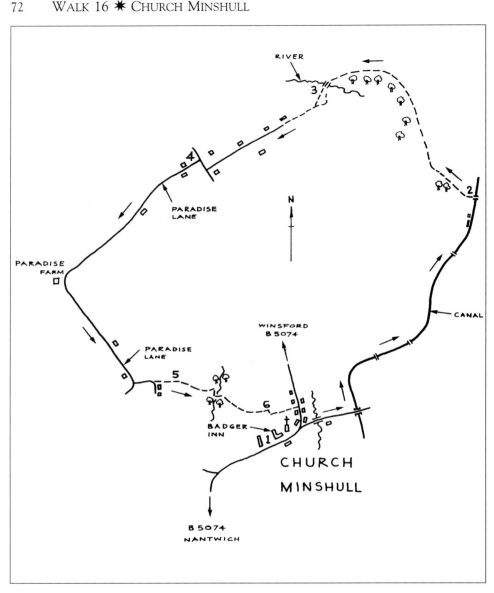

Follow Paradise Lane and after ¾ mile keep along the lane where it turns sharply to the left by Paradise Farm. Continue along the lane to where, in just under a further ½ mile, it turns sharply to the right. Turn left here, to enter a rough macadam lane which leads towards a dwelling and outbuildings. After 100 yards go over a stile at the side of a facing field gate. Follow a field edge and after 165 yards go over a stile in a crossing fence and hedgerow to enter a large field.

❺ Bear slightly right here and walk to a stile in a crossing fence about 330 yards away. On crossing the stile turn left to keep the fence on your immediate left. After 65 yards bear right and then go over a plank-bridge which takes you over a tree-lined stream. A stile in a crossing fence takes you into a large undulating field. Bear right now and climb across the field to converge with a track. Pass through a gateway and continue along the track. There is a hedgerow on the immediate right now – over which can be seen the tower of the church at Church Minshull. Descend along the track and then go over a stile at the right-hand side of the stump of a large tree.

❻ Turn right, then after 55 yards turn left, to follow a rough grassy divide between two fields. Go over a stile which is about 20 yards to the right of a dwelling and 6 yards to the left of an electricity pole. A short narrow hedged-in path leads to another stile. Cross the stile and turn right to follow the exit drive away from the dwelling, descending to a crossing road. Turn right now and follow the roadside pavement past attractive half-timbered dwellings back into Church Minshull.

The Shropshire Union Canal

ASHLEY

Length : 5 miles

Getting there: Ashley is situated on a minor road midway between the A538 and A556, 2 miles to the south of Hale. Access can be gained from either junction 6 or 7 of the M56 motorway.	**Parking:** There is a car park at the Greyhound Inn (for patrons). Alternatively there is a laneside parking area near Coppice Farm (GR 769855).	**Map:** OS Landranger – Manchester (109) (GR 775843).

A tiny village at the edge of the conurbation of Greater Manchester, Ashley has a post office, a church, a cricket pitch and a village pub. The surrounding area contains many scenic footpaths and popular beauty spots. One of the main attractions of the area is the river Bollin, whose waters flow peacefully through a wooded valley where wildlife abounds. Between the village and the Bollin there are many old farms and dwellings – the oldest being Ashley Hall, which dates from 1492.

The outward leg of the walk takes you past Ashley Hall and through the Bollin valley, prior to skirting the fringes of Bowdon. On the return journey the Bollin is once again traversed before returning to Ashley along footpaths and lanes through the lush green countryside of north-east Cheshire.

THE WALK

❶ From the Greyhound Inn turn right and enter Ashley Road – in the direction of Rostherne and Mere. Follow the roadside pavement, pass the post office, and cross over the railway via a road bridge. Keep on past the church and where the road bends to the left turn right to follow a lane which commences by South Lodge. The lane takes you over the motorway and leads past Ashley Hall – which is now part of a working farm. Shortly, over to the left, the tower of Bowdon church comes into view across the fields.

❷ Emerge at a bend in a crossing road and keep forward along the roadside pavement. Turn next left to enter a lane by Coppice Farm. On the right is an old tithe barn of cruck construction having heavy, weathered oak boarding which has remained in excellent condition.

A little further on there is a laneside parking area on the left (which is the

FOOD and DRINK

The Greyhound dates from the 18th century and is actually quite a bit larger than it appears. Originally called the Orrell Arms, the pub took its present name in 1841, when it became part of the Tatton estate. Owned by Greenalls, this attractive inn serves a wide variety of food lunchtime and evening every day of the week. Daily choices are displayed on a blackboard in the lounge area. During summertime there is a beer garden (tel: 0161 941 2246).

PLACES of INTEREST

The great park at **Tatton**, which is to the south-west of Ashley, gives a glimpse of a way of life which is hundreds of years old and contains a mansion and hall, a working farm and delightful gardens (tel: 01565 750250). Four miles to the east of Ashley, and to the north of Wilmslow, is the award winning museum at **Quarry Bank Mill**, where a 200 year old working environment has been recreated (tel: 01625 527468).

alternative parking area). Arrive at a junction. A track to the left goes to Ryecroft Farm, but keep right here to stay on the lane. Down on the right, through trees, is the first glimpse of the rippling waters of the river Bollin. The lane terminates at a dwelling called Ashley Mill. Keep to the right here to follow a footpath which descends and takes you over the river via a stout footbridge.

❸ Immediately on crossing the river, turn left to follow a footpath which stays along the riverside. Shortly, the river bends away to the left, but keep straight ahead here to follow a well-defined footpath. Go over a stream via a bridge made up of a number of broad flat planks. A facing track leads through trees and then climbs up widely spaced steps. A narrow gully takes you onto a path which is fenced-in on both sides. Across the fields on the right can be seen a mansion and adjacent church.

The path goes between dwellings and emerges onto a lane. Keep forward here to follow the facing lane. There is a sports field on the right now which belongs to Bowdon primary school. Continue past the school and then turn next left to walk along York Road.

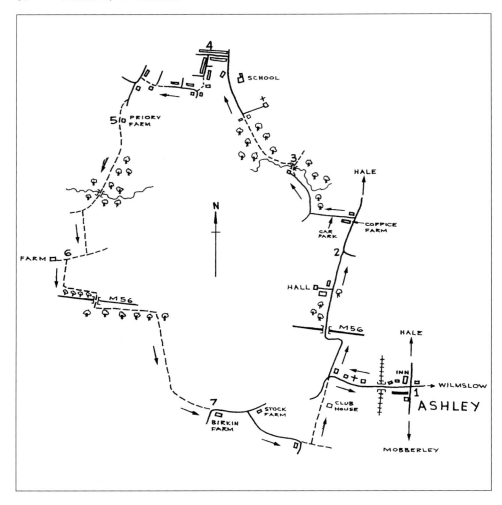

❹ Turn next left and enter Eaton Road. At the end of Eaton Road keep left to follow a macadam path into Birch Tree Close. Pass to the right of houses and emerge at a bend in a crossing road – the house on the immediate left is No 1. Turn right, follow the roadside pavement and, a little further on, enter Bailey Walk. Where Bailey Walk terminates, keep forward to enter a facing footpath which goes between dwellings. Pass the head of a road which goes off to the right and continue along the footpath. On the immediate left here is Bowdon Vale Cricket Club (BVCC). Pass between dwellings and emerge onto Bow Lane. Turn left, and where Bow Lane turns to the right, enter a facing lane at the side of Priory Lodges. After a further 90 yards, and 65 yards or so before arriving at a pair of gateposts, leave the lane to the right to follow a footpath which commences through a gap in a wooden fence. The footpath goes through trees at first and then takes you past Priory Farm with its ornate clock and weather-vane. A tablet set into the building tells you that the farm dates from 1786 and was rebuilt in 1990.

❺ From Priory Farm, follow a well-defined path which takes you across the facing field. Cross a stile which gives access to the next field and gradually descend. On crossing another stile continue along a facing path where there are trees on the left and a hedgerow on the right. Go over a footbridge which takes you over the river Bollin once again and then climb forward to follow a footpath which leads across a field and gradually converges with a hedgerow. There is a junction of paths now. Turn left to follow a straight path along a field edge, keeping a hedgerow on your immediate right. On meeting a crossing track turn right, to walk in the direction of a farm which can be seen about 275 yards away. About 90 yards before the farm is reached turn left to cross a stile which gives access to a field where a sign points to Birkinheath Lane and Ashley Road.

❻ Follow the field edge, keeping a hedgerow on your immediate left. Shortly, there is a small wood on the left. Go over a stile here to follow a path which skirts the edge of the wood. The path leads to a bridge which crosses the motorway. Immediately on crossing the motorway turn left to follow a path which stays parallel with the motorway. After 300 yards or so, the path turns to the right and leads onto a track along a field edge where there is a hedgerow on the left. Follow the track where it bends to the left and arrive at a crossing road via a stile at the side of a gate. Turn left to follow the roadside pavement.

❼ Pass Birkin Farm and Birkin Cottage. Turn next right, just before Stock Farm is reached, to enter Lamb Lane. The lane bends and climbs slightly. Where the lane turns sharply to the right by a dwelling, keep forward to go over a facing stile at the side of a field gate. Follow the field edge, keeping a hedgerow on your immediate left. After 110 yards, go over a stile on the left to enter another field. Walk forward now, in the direction of Ashley Cricket Club clubhouse, which can be seen about 300 yards away, straight ahead. Cross two further stiles and arrive on a track to the left of the clubhouse. A short length of facing track leads to a crossing road where the way is right.

You are now back on part of your initial route. A short stroll takes you back into Ashley village.

HOLMES CHAPEL

Length : 5 miles

Getting there: Holmes Chapel is at the junction of the A50 and A54 roads, 7 miles south of Knutsford. The village is just over 1 mile east of junction 18 of the M6 motorway.

Parking: If you are visiting the Old Red Lion Inn in the centre of the village next to the church, you may park in their car park. Alternatively, there are places in and around the village.

Map: OS Landranger – Stoke-on-Trent (118) (GR 763672).

Holmes Chapel is well known to motorists travelling along the A50 for its churchyard juts out to the edge of the road and care has to be exercised when driving past it. Although the village has expanded and is now a small town, it has many interesting buildings. St Luke's church has been altered over many cen- turies and contains some fine timber work. The adjacent Old Red Lion Inn, outside which John Wesley preached in 1738, is a fine example of a coaching inn. The church and the inn, together with a couple of adjacent cottages, were the only survivors of a fire which swept through the village on 10th July 1753.

The walk takes you away from the village and into the wide shallow valley of the river Dane. A scenic path takes you close to the river before climbing across farmland to more level terrain. The return leg is along paths, tracks and lanes and passes close to the massive structure of a brick railway viaduct before returning to Holmes Chapel along the banks of the river Dane.

THE WALK

❶ From the Old Red Lion Inn enter a lane which takes you around the rear of the church. Continue past a picturesque row of dwellings and on passing Church View (No 3) enter a narrow passageway, then emerge at a crossing road. Cross the road and turn right to follow the roadside pavement. After 1/4 mile turn left to walk along Hermitage Drive. Keep on past Rees Crescent and then descend past Elm Drive. Immediately on passing Danefield Road enter a facing track through a gate set between brick pillars. Descend, pass through a gate, then cross a stone bridge which takes you over the river Dane.

❷ Immediately on crossing the bridge go through a metal kissing-gate on the

---

PLACES of INTEREST

The world famous radio telescope at **Jodrell Bank** is only 4 miles to the north-east of Holmes Chapel and is reached via the A535 Holmes Chapel to Chelford road. There are space-age exhibitions and a wonderful arboretum on the site where children of all ages can learn about the Earth and the solar system of which it is a part. (The site telephone number is: 01477 571339.)

---

left. Walk forward across a rough pasture, keeping the river on your immediate left at first. After about 100 yards, the river turns away to the left, but keep forward here in the same general direction as before – aiming to the left of a large tree which can be seen about 275 yards away. Go over a stile in a crossing fence close to the riverside and keep on in the same direction as before. On passing close to a telegraph pole set in a hedgerow on the right, a building can be seen about 400 yards away straight ahead. Aim to the right of the building and cross a rough flat pasture. Pass over a stile at the side of a tree close to the riverside and then climb diagonally to the right to arrive in front of a stile which can be seen in a crossing hedgerow about 90 yards away.

❸ Do not cross the stile but turn right and continue, keeping the hedgerow on your immediate left, to go over two stiles in quick succession. Walk forward now, into a large undulating field, keeping a fence which is interspersed with hedges on your immediate left. After about 100 yards, the hedge on your left turns away to the left, but keep forward across the field in the

---

FOOD and DRINK

There are three inns and a Chinese restaurant in Holmes Chapel. The Old Red Lion Inn at the side of St Luke's church provides a wide selection of daily specials, bar meals, snacks and sandwiches – as well as liquid refreshment. Internally, the inn has many exposed beams and a spacious lounge with an open fire and wood panelling. The inn also has a beer garden (tel: 01477 532296).

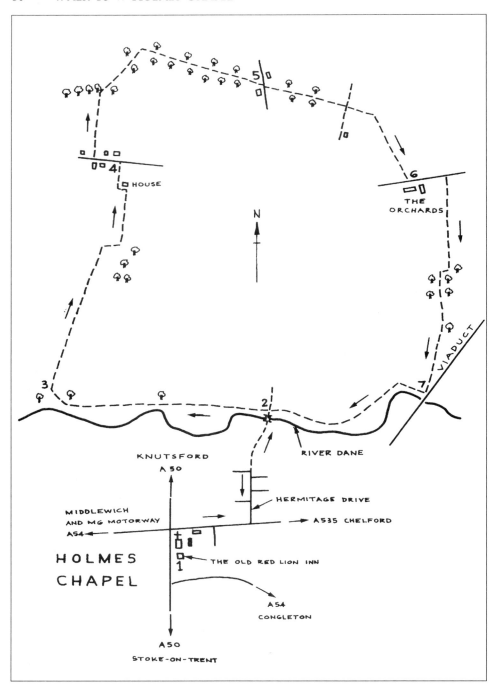

direction of a large house which can be seen about $1/2$ mile away in front of trees straight ahead. Pass over a stile in a crossing fence and hedgerow and climb up the facing field in the same general direction as before. On reaching a crossing fence and hedgerow turn right to where, after about 115 yards, there is a stile on the left. Cross the stile and immediately turn left through a field gate and then turn right to follow the edge of a large field keeping a hedgerow on your immediate right. Turn left on meeting a facing hedgerow – which forms the garden hedge of the house you used as your previous aiming point – and then go over a stile where the hedgerow finishes to follow a narrow hedged-in path. The path takes you onto the approach drive to the house. Follow the facing drive to arrive at a crossing lane.

❹ Turn left along the lane and pass various dwellings. About 275 yards after joining the lane go over a stile on the right – opposite an old barn and integral cottage. Cross two narrow fields via stiles and then continue towards a bank of facing trees which can be seen straight ahead about 200 yards away. Go over a stile at the edge of the trees and bear diagonally right. This area was once a large wood but many of the trees have been felled. After about 220 yards there is a fence on the immediate right which follows a row of silver birch trees. Pass between trees to arrive at a facing gate. Go over a stile on the right here, which takes you into trees. Follow a well-worn path which generally follows the course of a ditch on the right. Arrive at a crossing lane via a stile.

❺ Walk across the lane and continue along a path which still follows the course of a ditch on the right. Shortly, over to the right, the buildings of a large poultry farm can be seen through the trees. After about 350 yards arrive at a junction of paths. About 100 yards to the right there is a small dwelling – whilst on the immediate left there is a field gate. Go through the field gate and continue in the same general direction as before to a stile in a crossing hedgerow which can be seen about 150 yards away across the field. On crossing the stile follow a facing path and then go over a stile at the side of a telegraph pole. Join a facing track which leads towards a farm. Go through a gate and follow a concrete drive. A gate opposite the farm outbuildings gives access to a lane.

❻ Turn left along the lane. Pass the entrance to the farm – which is called The Orchards. The farm buildings are very interesting and contain a tower set amidst ornamental gardens. About 220 yards after passing the farm leave the lane through a field gate on the right. Follow the edge of a large field now, keeping a hedgerow on your immediate left. Across to the left, on the skyline, can be seen the hill and folly of Mow Cop. On reaching the end of the field turn right at facing trees and then turn left to descend. Go through a wooden kissing-gate and climb steps to walk along a grassy plateau between trees. The massive structure of a brick railway viaduct comes into view. The viaduct, which has 23 arches, carries the railway across the wide shallow valley of the river Dane at this point. Descend towards the right-hand end of the viaduct, passing to the right of an isolated tree. Arrive close by the viaduct at a point where the river Dane passes under it. There is a facing stile at the base of one of the supporting arches here.

❼   Do not cross the stile but turn sharply to the right and walk away from the viaduct, keeping the river on your immediate left. Go over a wooden footbridge at the field corner and then climb up a low bank to enter a large field. The river turns away to the left here but keep forward, bearing left, to converge with the river again after about 275 yards where a stile takes you over a crossing fence. Follow the course of the river now and arrive at a stone bridge via a stile. Turn left and cross the bridge.

You are now back on part of your initial route. Climb along the facing track to join Hermitage Drive. On reaching the crossroads ahead turn right for the short stroll back into Holmes Chapel.

Hermitage Bridge – across the river Dane

MOBBERLEY

Length : 3 miles

Getting there: Mobberley straddles the B5085 between Knutsford and Wilmslow. The road dips through a hollow on the Wilmslow side of the village at a junction with Church Lane. Drive along Church Lane and after ¼ mile arrive at the Church Inn.

Parking: There are parking places in and around the village. There is also a car park at the side of the Church Inn for those visiting the pub.

Map: OS Landranger – Manchester (109) and Stoke-on-Trent (118) (GR 791802).

Mobberley can boast a long history, going back centuries before its mention in the Domesday Book. The village possesses many attractive and interesting buildings of varied styles which are a delight to the discerning visitor. There is also a splendid church, dedicated to St Wilfrid, which dates back to 1245. Close by the church is the cricket pitch where local players test their skills on summer Sunday afternoons. On the fringes of the village is Mobberley Old Hall whose mullioned windows have gazed out across the surrounding countryside since 1612.

The walk initially follows cross-country paths and lanes to the scenic hamlet of

Knolls Green. The return leg is along a delightful path which never strays too far away from the bubbling waters of Mobberley Brook.

THE WALK

❶ The walk commences from the Church Inn, over a stile at the side of a field gate set in the hedgerow which surrounds the car park. Having crossed the stile, bear diagonally right and cross a field to pass the corner of a small sports field. Arrive at the field corner and go through a wooden kissing-gate. Follow the edge of the next field, keeping a hedgerow on your immediate left. Pass over a stile at the field corner and continue along the edge of the next field, keeping a hedgerow which is interspersed with trees on your immediate right. Keep on, past a footpath which goes off to the right and then pass over a stile to the right of a dwelling. Follow a track now, which takes you close to outbuildings. Pass through gates and keep forward along a hedged-in track. Pass a delightful brick-built farmhouse on the left. The track becomes a macadam lane and takes you

---

FOOD and DRINK

The Church Inn, a charming place, serves food every lunchtime and during the evening, Monday to Saturday inclusive. On Sunday food is only served at lunchtime. Snacks, bar meals or full restaurant meals can be purchased – the house speciality being rib of beef (tel: 01565 872651). A short distance from the Church Inn, and on the route of the return leg of the walk, are the Bull's Head and the Roebuck; both offer a wide range of food and drink. Halfway around the walk, at Knolls Green, is the Bird in Hand Inn which is situated at just the right place for a refreshing drink.

PLACES of INTEREST

Just over 2 miles from Mobberley, and reached via the B5085, is the delightful town of **Knutsford**. The town is the setting of Mrs Gaskell's 'Cranford' and many buildings which would have been familiar to her remain. There are many fine Georgian buildings and a wide choice of attractive shops. During recent years the Heritage Centre has been restored and features regular exhibitions of local interest and crafts.

---

past a dwelling called Andar and then to a crossing road.

❷ Go over the road and turn left to follow the roadside pavement. Pass Oak House (1872) and Mobberley Riding School, to where, about 115 yards further on, there is a stile on the right at the left-hand side of a field gate. Cross the stile and walk along a field edge, keeping a fence, and then a hedgerow, on the immediate left. Go over a stile at the field corner and continue along the edge of the next field. Cross a stile about 10 yards to the right of the field corner. Turn left and after about 20 yards turn right at the field corner and continue along the field edge, keeping a hedgerow on your immediate left. Pass over a stile set in a facing hedgerow at the field corner and follow the edge of the next field. After only 90 yards go over a stile in a crossing fence and continue along the edge of the next field. After a further 115 yards a stile at the side of a field gate takes you onto a crossing lane.

❸ Turn right along the lane and pass dwellings called Moss Croft and Moss Lea. Immediately on passing the entrance drive of Yew Tree Farm arrive at a junction of

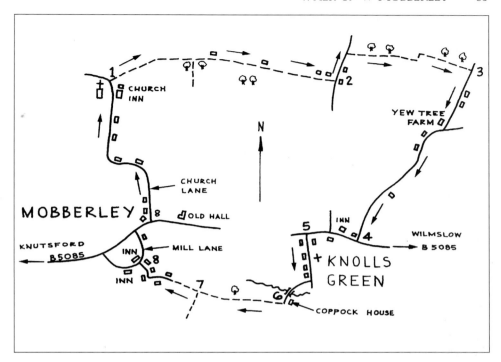

lanes, where the way is right. Pass a bungalow called Annapurna. The lane winds past other dwellings and leads to a crossing road.

❹ Turn right and follow the roadside pavement. Pass The Old Chapel, a dwelling which was once a church, and enter the hamlet of Knolls Green. On the right is the Bird in Hand Inn where refreshment can be obtained if required. Cross the road now, taking care, and continue along the roadside pavement. On the left there is a bakery which dates back many years. Keep on, in the direction of Knutsford, ignoring a road on the right which goes to Morley Green and Styal. After a further 220 yards turn left to enter Faulkners Lane.

❺ Pass the Methodist church and 130 yards further on, enter a rough macadam drive on the right which commences at the side of a dwelling called Merrydale. There is a footpath sign at the head of this drive and a board indicating Coppock House. Follow the drive over Mobberley Brook and then pass Coppock House. Go through a facing gate and turn right to walk to a stile at the side of a field gate.

❻ Cross the stile and follow a field edge, keeping a hedgerow on your immediate right. At the field corner, go over a stile at the side of a gate and continue, again keeping a hedgerow on your immediate right. On reaching the field corner, go over a plank-bridge and stile. Climb up a facing bank to enter a large field. Bear slightly right now, and cross the field. Arrive at a facing track – where there is also a path going off to the left which climbs between hedges.

❼ Walk forward along the facing track which generally follows level terrain. The track becomes a macadam lane. Keep forward now, to follow the lane as it winds past dwellings and arrive at a junction opposite the Bull's Head (a few yards to the left there is another inn called the Roebuck). Turn right and pass in front of the Bull's Head to follow the laneside pavement. This is Mill Lane, which shortly leads to a crossing road. Go over the road, taking care as it is usually quite busy, and turn right to follow a roadside path which gradually climbs where there are railings at its right-hand side. After 130 yards arrive at Church Lane, which goes off to the left.

The way is along Church Lane but first of all it is well worth walking a few more yards along Hall Lane to have a look at the fine building of Mobberley Old Hall, which dates from 1612. (The Hall is a private dwelling but its magnificence can be observed from the roadside.)

❽ Enter Church Lane. On the left here is the Victory Hall, which was built to commemorate the end of the First World War and is used by the villagers for all sorts of activities and functions. Follow the laneside pavement and pass the attractive building of Slade Cottage. The lane winds past Mobberley Cricket Club, opposite which is the aptly named Cover Point, a private dwelling. On the left shortly there is a path which leads to the church, which you may wish to look around before returning to the car park (across the road from the church).

Looking back to the village on the way to Knolls Green

EATON

Length : 5¹/₂ miles

<table>
<tr><td>Getting there: Eaton straddles the A536 Congleton to Macclesfield road 2 miles to the north-east of Congleton.

Parking: There is a car park</td><td>at the Plough Inn (for patrons) situated in the centre of the village just off the A536. Alternatively, there are parking places in and around the village.</td><td>Map: OS Landranger – Stoke-on-Trent (118) (GR 870655).</td></tr>
</table>

At the heart of a magnificent tract of countryside and close to the winding river Dane, Eaton is a small village containing a mixture of old dwellings and more modern houses and bungalows. It has a small church and an impressive inn, the Plough, which was originally built as a coaching inn during the 17th century.

The outward leg of the walk leads away from the village and follows a cross-country path which is never too far away from the river Dane. A short section of lane then takes you into the hamlet of North Rode. The route crosses parkland before returning to Eaton along a series of minor lanes.

THE WALK

❶ From the Plough, walk forward to the main road and turn left to follow the roadside pavement. The pavement climbs and passes between hedgerows but stays parallel to the main road. Where the pavement finishes, turn right, cross the road – taking care as it is usually quite busy – and enter a footpath which begins close by a dwelling. A sign here says 'Public Footpath – North Rode'. Pass over a stile near to the dwelling and then go through a gap to enter a large field. Keep forward, passing to the left of a row of large trees and descend to go over a plank-bridge and stile. Cross the next field in the same general direction as before, passing to the left of a telegraph pole. Keep to the right of a facing hedgerow and continue along the field edge, keeping a hedgerow on your immediate left. Go over a stile at the field corner and shortly turn right, through a gap in

---

FOOD and DRINK

At the Plough no expense has been spared in creating an establishment of the highest quality. The elegant traditional furnishings, oak beams and glowing log fires in winter, reflect the tranquil warmth and friendly atmosphere of its peaceful rural setting. The owners are justly proud of the inn's reputation for its food – which is prepared to satisfy the most discerning palate. The emphasis is towards French cuisine, although there is also a wide general choice which is supplemented by a daily specials board. There is also an inspiring selection of fine beers and wines. Outside, there is a play area for children, a lawn with bench seats and tables, and a stable block which has been converted into individual bedrooms. The Plough is open seven days a week for lunch and dinner, including a traditional carvery all day Sunday (it is advisable to book at weekends – tel: 01260 280207).

PLACES of INTEREST

Just over 3 miles to the north-east of Eaton, and lying close to the A536, is the village of Gawsworth. There are attractive dwellings here and a splendid church, set close to a lake. The main attraction, though, is **Gawsworth Hall**. The origins of the present Hall date back to the 15th century and it is still very much a family home, full of warmth and charm. The Hall and gardens are open to the public from late March to early October from 2 pm to 5 pm daily (tel: 01260 223456).

---

gorse bushes, to descend to an old plank-bridge at the side of a large oak tree.

❷ Cross the plank-bridge and enter a large undulating field. Walk forward, passing close to an isolated tree, and on nearing the end of the field, descend and pass over a footbridge which is set in bushes. Proceed, keeping along the lower ground, and then go over a plank-bridge after which you gradually converge with a fence on the right. Keep on past a field gate and follow a field edge, keeping a hedge and fence on your immediate right, and go over a couple of stiles. Cross the next field in the direction of a mast which can be seen on top of the facing Croker Hill – which dominates the skyline straight ahead. Another stile gives access to a large field. Walk forward, in the same general direction as before, to arrive at the corner of a hedgerow.

❸ Bear diagonally right now, keeping the hedgerow on your immediate right, to walk towards the left-hand end of a railway viaduct which can be seen across the fields. From this part of the footpath there is a fine view of The Cloud, a large hill which

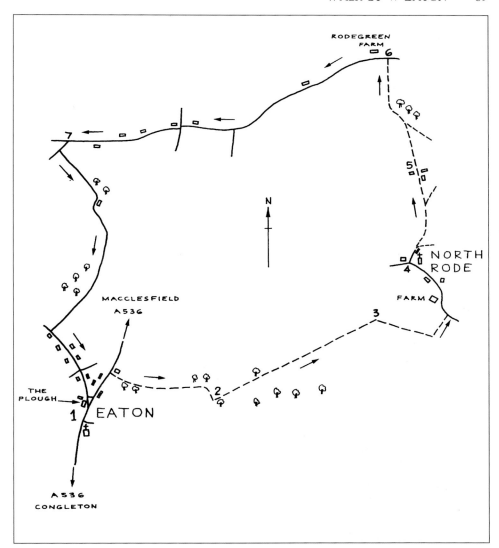

dominates the skyline over to the right.

Pass a couple of field gates and then go over a stile at the field corner. Walk forward for 10 yards or so, and then turn left, to walk up a long field, keeping a hedgerow on the left about 10 yards away. Go through a facing gate at the end of the field and join a crossing lane. Turn left and follow the lane as it winds and climbs into the hamlet of North Rode.

❹ Enter a lane on the right which commences between the church and The Daintry Hall (1835). After 90 yards, go through a facing gateway, pass Lodge Cottage, and continue along a macadam driveway. About 55 yards further on, there is a junction of ways. Bear left here, over a cattle-grid, and walk along a concrete driveway; the driveway takes you through a parkland setting, where there are fine views across the surrounding countryside. Ignore a gravel track which goes off to the right and then pass over a cattle-grid close by a dwelling. Keep forward now, to go over a facing stile at the right-hand side of a field gate between outbuildings.

❺ Follow a facing grassy track, which gradually bends to the left, and then join a more well-defined track in front of facing trees. Continue, and then go over a stile at the side of a gate. The track leads to a lane via a stile at the side of a gate.

❻ Turn left and follow the lane past Rodegreen Farm. Keep on past a pair of cottages and about $1/2$ mile further on keep right in the direction of Marton. The lane narrows and leads to a crossing road. Cross the road – taking care as it is usually quite busy – and enter the facing Cocksmoss Lane. About $1/2$ mile further on arrive at a junction of lanes.

❼ Bear left here, then, after only 90 yards, turn left at the next junction to enter a narrow lane. Follow this typical Cheshire lane for $3/4$ mile to arrive at a junction on the outskirts of the village of Eaton. Turn left now, to follow the laneside pavement back into the village.

KETTLESHULME

Length : 6 miles

Getting there: The B5470 links Whaley Bridge with Rainow and Macclesfield. The village of Kettleshulme straddles this road about 2 miles from Whaley Bridge.

Parking: Because parking locations within the village are at a premium, the walk commences from Pym Chair car park. This is reached by climbing out of Kettleshulme along a lane which leaves the B5470 near to the village school and is headed by a sign to Goyt Valley and Dunge Valley Gardens. After ³/₄ mile keep straight on at a crossroads and continue climbing to where just over 1 mile further on, Pym Chair car park is reached, on the left. The car park is about 100 yards before a junction of lanes (if the car park is full there is a parking layby down the lane to the right).

Map: OS Landranger – Stoke-on-Trent (118) (GR 995768).

Situated within the Peak District National Park, Kettleshulme is at the heart of some marvellous scenery. The village was first recorded in 1285 and is on the route of the old Salt Way which passed through Nantwich and Middlewich before crossing the hills of the Peak District to Sheffield and Chesterfield. During the 18th century, both silk and cotton were woven in local cottages and the nearby Todd Brook was utilised to drive a waterwheel for a small spinning and weaving mill. Today, horticulture and farming are the main activities pursued by the villagers – who are justifiably proud of their local community.

This is hilly country, where the effort of climbing is rewarded with delightful panoramic views in all directions. From Pym Chair car park the route is along a concessionary path that gradually descends to Windgather Rocks. A cross-country path then descends to Kettleshulme. The return leg of the walk takes you along the valley of the Todd Brook to Jenkin Chapel – followed by a steep climb along a lane which leads back to the car park.

THE WALK

❶ On leaving the car park turn left and follow the laneside verge to the junction of lanes. Turn left again, in the direction of Buxton, to continue along the laneside verge. Go over a stile on the left now, about 45 yards past a footpath which goes off to the right. Follow a well-worn path through banks of heather and gradually descend. The path leads to a stile by a lane. Do not cross this stile but bear right to follow a

---

PLACES of INTEREST

Dunge Valley Gardens are situated at Dunge Farm, access to which is along a track signed off the lane between Pym Chair car park and Kettleshulme. The site contains a wide variety of unusual perennials and shrubs within a magnificent setting. Plants can be purchased and there is a tea-room. The site is open daily from the beginning of April until the end of August (tel: 01663 733787).

---

concessionary path which stays parallel with the lane, which can be seen over a stone wall on the immediate left. Go over a stile in a crossing fence and continue over rough terrain to gradually climb to the rear of the cliffs formed by Windgather Rocks. Take care here, as the drop to the left is quite sheer. At the highest point, stop to admire wonderful panoramic views in all directions.

❷ Continue to a crossing stone wall, turn right, and then go over a stile. Descend towards trees where there is a stone wall on the left and a fence on the right. Turn left with the wall and follow the edge of the trees, keeping the wall on your immediate left. On crossing a stile, turn right through less densely planted trees and descend along the edge of the dense fenced-in wood. At the bottom of the descent go over a plank-bridge and climb forward in the same general direction as before, keeping the dense fenced-in wood on the right. Turn sharply to the right at the end of the wood and, after a further 55 yards, go over a tall step-stile. Climb forward here, keeping a stone wall on the left and after only 25 yards, go over a stile set in the wall. A generally level path leads towards a farm

---

FOOD and DRINK

Kettleshulme has two pubs: the Bull's Head and the Swan. The latter does not serve food, but the Bull's Head provides sandwiches on Saturdays and meals every Sunday at lunchtime and during the evening. Opposite the Bull's Head is the Tea Cosy, where morning coffee, light lunches and afternoon teas can be purchased. All three establishments have small adjacent car parks (for patrons).

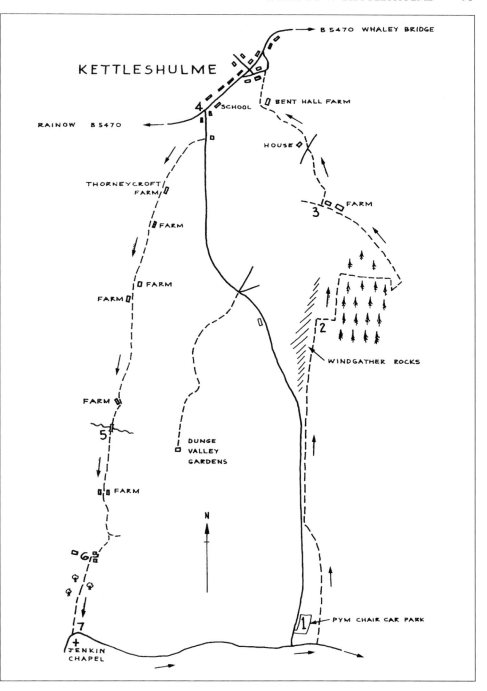

KETTLESHULME

B 5470 WHALEY BRIDGE

BENT HALL FARM

4 SCHOOL

RAINOW   B 5470

HOUSE

THORNEYCROFT
FARM

FARM

3   FARM

FARM

FARM   FARM

2

WINDGATHER ROCKS

FARM

5

DUNGE
VALLEY
GARDENS

FARM

N

6

7

JENKIN
CHAPEL

1   PYM CHAIR CAR PARK

which can be seen about 300 yards away straight ahead. There is a stone wall on the immediate left for part of the way. Go through a facing gateway and follow a track to a gate. Keep to the left of this gate and then go over a stile set in a stone wall directly in front of the farmhouse. Immediately on crossing this stile turn left over a second stile and follow the farm approach track past the entrance to Blackhill Gate Cottage. Only 55 yards farther on, a footpath commences on the right.

❸ Go over a step-stile here, then pass through a gate to follow a field edge. Pass through another gate and go over a stile. Gradually descend across the next field and go over a stile about 100 yards away. Bear slightly left now, to descend across a field in the direction of a dwelling which can be seen down in a hollow about 275 yards away. A stile at the side of a field gate gives access to a crossing lane, where the way is right. After only 45 yards, leave the lane to the left over a stile which is at the right-hand side of the entrance drive to the dwelling mentioned above. An obvious path takes you along the right-hand side of a small valley. Go over a fence-stile and keep forward through a rough field. The path converges with a hedge on the right and a line of electricity poles. Pass to the right of a field gate and keep on along the path, which is never too far away from the electricity poles. Where the poles finish, the path descends more steeply past gorse bushes. Go over a stile, cross a brook, and then climb to go over a stile in a stone wall. Continue, keeping a wall on the right, and join a facing track. Go through a gate, pass a dwelling, and turn right to follow the track past the entrance to Bent Hall Farm. Descend along the track to arrive at a crossing lane. Turn left now to walk into the village of Kettleshulme.

The village contains numerous sturdily built cottages – many having attractive gardens which are a delight during the summer months. Close by is the Bull's Head Inn and the Tea Cosy, where thirst and hunger can be satisfied. Further down to the right, past the library, is the tiny building of the Swan Inn, opposite which there is a garden centre set within large ornamental gardens.

❹ Having looked around the village, enter a lane which commences just past the village school where a sign points to Goyt Valley and Dunge Valley Gardens. Climb along the lane and, after 220 yards, turn right to enter a track which begins opposite the entrance to a bungalow. Pass through Thorneycroft Farm and continue along a generally level track. Pass through a working farm and continue. The track takes you past another couple of farms. On passing the second farm the track terminates at a facing gate. Go through the gate and follow a path along a line of telegraph poles at the left edge of a field. Go over a stile at the end of the field and continue with a fence on the immediate right in the same general direction as before along a level path. At the field corner go over a stile in a stone wall and keep on, in the direction of a farm which can be seen about 150 yards away straight ahead. Immediately on passing the farmhouse go over a stile on the right which is only 2 yards past the gable end of the farmhouse. Having crossed this stile turn left through a gap and bear diagonally right to cross a rough pasture through tussocks to arrive at a stout wooden footbridge which takes you over a stream.

❺ Climb up a facing bank and after only 15 yards go over a stile in a crossing fence. Follow the edge of a very large field now, keeping a fence, and then trees, on your immediate left. Go over a stile in a crossing fence and walk straight across a field in the direction of a farm about 275 yards away, half-hidden by trees. Just before reaching the farm buildings, go over a stile in a crossing fence and turn right to pass through three gates. Walk between farm buildings and then keep to the left of a raised flower bed to follow a track which leads away from the farm. Where the track turns sharply to the left, keep forward to go over a stile and then go over a footbridge. Follow a field edge now, keeping a hawthorn hedge, and other trees, on your immediate left. The path hugs a stone wall on the left and takes you to a gate at the left-hand side of derelict buildings. Go through the gate, turn right between the buildings, and then left to pass through a facing gateway.

❻ Only 3 yards after passing through the gateway the track turns to the right. Do not follow the track as it turns to the right, but climb up a facing bank to enter a rough pasture. Walk across a rough thistle-strewn area interspersed with hawthorn trees. Arrive at a gate in a crossing fence – from where the stark stone bell tower and adjoining building of Jenkin Chapel can be seen across a facing field about 300 yards away. Go through the gate and walk across the field, aiming to the right of Jenkin Chapel, and converge with a stone wall on the left. Go over a stile at the field corner and arrive at a junction of lanes close by Jenkin Chapel. The way is left to climb along the lane which goes to Goyt Valley and Kettleshulme, but first of all take a look at Jenkin Chapel.

Local farmers finished construction of the chapel in 1733. Built to withstand the harsh upland climate of this part of Cheshire, the chapel has a heavy slab roof which is supported by thick solid walls. The bell tower is reached by an outside flight of stone steps, whilst internally there are simple box pews and a high octagonal pulpit.

❼ Enter the lane which climbs towards Goyt Valley and Kettleshulme. A steep climb approaching $3/4$ mile leads to a junction of lanes. Turn left and arrive back at Pym Chair car park on the right.